THE WAY OF THE PHYSICIAN

ALSO BY JACOB NEEDLEMAN

The Heart of Philosophy (1982)

Consciousness and Tradition (1982)

Lost Christianity (1980)

Speaking of My Life (editor) (1979)

Understanding the New Religions (1978)
(editor, with George Baker)

On the Way to Self Knowledge (1976)
(editor, with Dennis Lewis)

A Sense of the Cosmos (1975)

Sacred Tradition and Present Need (1974)
(editor, with Dennis Lewis)

The Sword of Gnosis (editor) (1974)

Religion for a New Generation (1973)
(editor, with A.K. Bierman and James A.Gould)

The New Religions (1970)

Being-in-the-World (1963)

The Way of the Physician

JACOB NEEDLEMAN

1817

Harper & Row, Publishers, San Francisco
Cambridge, Hagerstown, New York, Philadelphia
London, Mexico City, São Paulo, Singapore, Sydney

FIRST EDITION

Library of Congress Cataloging in Publication Data

Needleman, Jacob.
    THE WAY OF THE PHYSICIAN.

    1. Physicians—Psychology. 2. Medical personnel—Attitudes. 3. Medicine—Philosophy. I. Title.
R727.8.N44 1985   610.69'52   84-48776
ISBN 0-06-250644-7

85 86 87 88 89 RRD 10 9 8 7 6 5 4 3 2 1

Contents

Acknowledgments

I have many people to thank, starting with Dr. Martin Brotman, director of education at Pacific Medical Center, and Dr. Bruce Spivey, president of Pacific Medical Center, whose invitation to conduct a series of seminars brought me into direct contact with the forces at work in modern medicine. Although the people and situations portrayed in this book have been fictionalized, much of the material in Part II is based on what I learned through leading these seminars and through the generous participation of the medical, nursing, and administrative staff, including Dr. William S. Andereck, Jr., Dr. Keith Cohn, Ms. Marybeth Flower, Dr. Barry Levin, Ms. Valerie Oblath, Mr. Aubrey Serfling, Dr. Leonard Shlain, Dr. Robert Szarnicki, and Dr. Dwight Wilbur. I am indebted to Dr. Levin for his ongoing support and for his wise observations about the role of technology in medicine, which I have made liberal use of, especially in chapter thirteen. I am similarly grateful to Mr. Serfling and to Dr. Andereck for their pointed observations about the impact of broad societal issues on the individual physician.

I am extremely grateful to Dr. Martin Lipp for bringing his uniquely humane perspective to these seminars and for writing two books, *Respectful Treatment* and *The Bitter Pill*, which helped open my eyes to the inner life of today's physician. I have made extensive use of Dr. Lipp's ideas in the chapters on "care" in this book. In general, I have constructed fictional characters in Part II to insure that the reader attribute the shortcomings in that section of the book to the inventions of the author rather than to the people who have helped me so much.

I am very grateful to Leona Butler both for her participation in the seminars and for her careful and penetrating reading of this book in manuscript. I have received a great deal of help for my own understanding from my personal and professional association with Dr. Albert R. Jonsen, Chief of the Division of Medical Ethics at the University of California Medical Center, and from conversations with Dr. Neil Halfon, also of the University of California Medical Center, who read portions of this book in manuscript. To my longtime friend, Dr. Laurens P. White, I owe thanks for countless down-to-earth conversations about the realities of medicine in all its aspects. To Dr. Jon Rothenberg I owe special thanks for the kind of criticism that I had almost given up hope of finding again.

My thanks also to John Loudon at Harper and Row who over the years has been a friend, a sensitive critic, and, now, a most supportive editor.

To Regina Eisenberg, Olivia Byrne, and Stephen Damon, who continue to help me so much and in so many ways, and to my great friend and literary agent, Marlene Gabriel, and to other companions not named, please accept yet one more inadequate expression of gratitude. Finally, I thank my wife, Carla, who supported this work through every kind of vicissitude.

Prologue: The Second Serpent

Everyone recognizes the staff encircled by two serpents. Known as the *caduceus* or *staff of Hermes*, it is universally identified as the emblem of the physician. Yet few of us are aware of its meaning or its strange place in the history of medicine. Scholars say it is fraudulent. The proper symbol of medicine, they insist, is the ancient *rod of Asclepius* with its single coiled serpent. Pointing out that the staff of Hermes came into widespread use only after its somewhat arbitrary adoption by the U.S. Army at the turn of the century, they vehemently maintain it has nothing whatever to do with the time-honored traditions of medicine.

Why, then, is the staff of Hermes on the cover of this book? The answer to this question lies in the real meaning of this ancient symbol: in the fact that there are two serpents, rather than one, and in the mysterious wings that hover above them. In this symbol we can read not only the key to a rebirth of the art of medicine but also the key to the art of living itself in our threatened and bewildered civilization. Through the idea represented by this symbol, we can see with new eyes the trap that is closing in around the contemporary physician and around each one of us. We can see quite precisely why the meaning of our own lives is slipping away from us. And we will find that the steps that can lead the physician out of this trap are the same steps that can lead each of us toward a real life of our own. In this sense, we are all physicians.

But, what is this staff of Hermes and where does it come from?

Historically speaking, Western medicine traces its roots back to ancient Greece, where the cult of Asclepius, the god of medicine, originated in the fifth century B.C. For nearly a thousand years sick and afflicted pilgrims flocked to the Grecian temples of

Asclepius to take part in a ritual called incubation. The ancient god of medicine was expected to visit them during a dream state and heal them or prescribe modes of treatment. More than 200 such temples existed, and throughout the ages the power of medicine was represented in the Western world by an image of this god holding in his hand the rod and serpent, symbolizing the power and wisdom that acts through nature itself. It is this symbol that the historians of medicine tell us is authentic.

However, another influence was entering into the life of ancient Greece at the same time as the arising of the cult of Asclepius. This was the teaching of Pythagoras, with its extraordinary blend of spiritual vision and scientific method, and its understanding of the human soul as a reconciler of the fundamental forces that clash and blend within the whole of the cosmos. Due, in part, to the influence of Pythagoras there arose the school of the great physician Hippocrates, the father of scientific medicine.

In late antiquity, however, when Christianity began its triumphal spread throughout Asia Minor and the European continent, mankind was turned away from the ancient emphasis on the power of nature. The Church turned toward God, the source of nature itself. More and more, nature and its great forces were ignored or even despised.

The cult of Asclepius was ultimately defeated. The mastery of nature, as represented by the rod and single serpent, was no longer revered. Man was to be led out of nature toward God above. But although the Asclepian vision of man's relationship to nature was eclipsed, the influence of Pythagoras survived as an underground current breaking through to the surface at certain key moments in history. This influence, this understanding of cosmic nature, has existed under many names. We know it best by the designation *Hermeticism*, just that teaching about man and nature associated with the ancient god Hermes!

During the Middle Ages and at the beginning of the modern era, the followers of this teaching called themselves *alchemists* and cloaked their ideas in a highly sophisticated code that turned man's attention directly to the several forces of nature and their action within the human psyche. Although numerous charlatans later assumed the name of alchemist, the authentic representatives of this teaching were concerned with one thing and one thing only: the transformation of human nature by means of an inner search that brought the mind into an exalted relationship to the great energies of Creation itself. The charlatan alchemists wrapped themselves in a materialistic fantasy of transmuting base metals into gold; the authentic alchemists sought to transmute corrupted human nature, symbolized by lead, into the "gold" of a fully developed spiritual consciousness.

The staff of Hermes was one of the principal symbols of this work of self-perfection. The two serpents represent the two fundamental forces of universal nature—one moving outward, away from the Source and the second moving back toward union with the Source. The world of nature was understood as the stage where these two opposing forces constantly war with each other. Out of this warfare the whole of the created world arises through the mediation and reconciliation of a third movement symbolized by the figure of a dove resting atop the staff in between the heads of the serpents. In some later representations we find the dove replaced by a pair of wings. In Christian terminology, this reconciling principle had been known under the name "the holy spirit."

Hermeticism carried with it a deep respect for the study of natural forces and the elements of the material world through which these forces manifest themselves. Thus, in the sixteenth and seventeenth centuries the staff of Hermes begins to appear as a printer's emblem in medicopharmaceutical texts. It is very likely that modern pharmacology owes its existence to the extraordinary attention given by the alchemists to the chemical elements of nature. But the Hermeticists' reverence for nature was to have a far greater impact on Western civilization than this. The arising of modern science itself owes much of its impetus to the Hermeticism of the late Renaissance. Francis Bacon, Johannes Kepler, and even the great Isaac Newton were inspired and guided by the Hermetic teachings about natural forces.

The roots of modern science thus lie embedded in a profound

system of spiritual metaphysics that in turn traces its own origin as far back as recorded history. Archaeologists have found a silver healing cup of the ancient Sumerians dating back to the year 2200 B.C.—the cup bears the image of the caduceus!

But although science began in this way, its development up to our time is quite another story. The view of nature offered by contemporary science bears no resemblance to that of the Hermeticists. The picture it presents of the forces of nature no longer carries hope for the spiritual and moral perfection of man. Nature is now seen as blind and mechanical; the cosmos is relentlessly moving downward toward universal death under the sway of the law of entropy. The idea of a second, evolving force opposed to this is nowhere acknowledged as intrinsic to the structure of creation, far less a third, reconciling force that brings these two "serpents" into harmonious balance.

Entrapped in this single-visioned relationship to nature, the teachings of science have depressed the culture of our contemporary world. The fathers of modern science were quickened by a vision of cosmic law as the dialectical workings of a universal Heart and Mind that penetrated the movements of the material world, including, of course, the human body. Their descendants, the representatives of the contemporary scientific world view, see only one basic movement, one fundamental direction in the whole of the cosmic scheme—a movement toward death, which can be masked but never conquered by the achievements of technology. There is no second serpent, and without the second serpent there cannot descend upon human life that energy universally symbolized by the wings of the dove and experienced as *meaning*.

The fate of medicine in the contemporary era is testimony to the teaching contained in the symbol of the caduceus. The meaning of the art of medicine, like the very meaning of being alive, cannot be found through one force alone. When the contemporary physician complains that the meaning of his craft is being taken away from him—by such mundane influences as government intervention, legal restrictions, hospital data banks, and insurance companies—we need to hear this complaint in a special way, because it is the same for all of us. More and more, we are all becoming aware that our lives are being lived for us by influences that, however numerous they appear, are in fact only so many reflections of one kind of movement in the life of man, a movement toward externals, toward needs and gratifications that, however justified in their own right, become destructive when they pretend to represent the whole meaning of human life.

The aim of this book is to demonstrate that the meaning of being a physician can only be recovered through a rediscovery of the question of the meaning of human life itself, the meaning of being alive. Like the faint light from a distant star, the ancient symbol of the caduceus has somehow managed to penetrate the atmosphere of our modern culture. No matter that the symbol has been used until now without our understanding its significance. Faced with the dissolution of the values that have formed the basis of our civilization, we are now in a position to study what the caduceus tells us about the meaning of our lives. Just as sensitive new scientific instruments enable us to perceive the hitherto unknown physical properties of distant suns, so the depth of our present need can make us more sensitive to the hitherto unknown power of great and ancient teachings about man in the universal world.

What are these two serpents? What is the struggle that can give authentic meaning and power to what we do and how we live?

A NOTE TO THE READER

With the exception of the author, Dr. Louis B. Fierman, and historical figures, all names, characteristics, and background details in the book have been changed. In addition, several figures in the book are wholly fictitious.

I. THE DREAM OF THE GREAT PHYSICIAN

1. The Good Doctor

I see you now as I saw you when I was very young. I am frightened by something that is happening in me. There is pain and weariness. I seem unable to think and I don't know what I am or what my body is doing to me.

Then you appear in my room. I remember your voice, quiet and strong. Never in my house was a voice so quiet, so free of agitation. Immediately, I feel something quiet in myself, some movement of opening and letting go. Alongside the fear and self-pity, there is now something inside me that is not afraid. Suddenly, I am two: a frightened child and a watchful presence.

You take my hand. I remember the pressure of your fingers around my wrist. I remember how you looked at me. No one ever looked at me like that. What were you seeing? Why did your look make me feel that I was in the world of men, not children?

Now you are exploring my body—mouth, eyes, chest. You turn me on my side and place the cold stethoscope against my back. What is there to listen for there? You turn me back again and lower the blankets. I am surprised that I feel no embarrassment. I watch your face as you probe and press, firmly, gently, sharply. When you cause pain, I make a sound, but without anger or hurt. With no one else do I react to pain in that way, simply as something physical, without emotion. Even when I'm alone, pain makes me emotional. But now I am only a watchful presence and a physical body. The frightened child, with nothing to feed on, has disappeared.

Your face is full of attention, full of listening. How I remember that face! No one ever looked at me or my body with such a face. How you trusted your power of listening, your state of attention. And how your trust brought into our house and into myself a movement toward a new order. I know now that this is why you devoted yourself to medicine even though you yourself didn't realize it. I know now that in your face so full of listening there was something a little bit like divinity, something I can now call love. But no one calls that love now. What stupid names people give it when it appears! We didn't call it love then, either; all we could do was to revere the role of the physician because down deep we sometimes sensed the mystery of that trust in total attention, the only thing in man that can meet life and death squarely, without cringing.

You pull the blankets up and stand over me. Gently you return me to the world of children and to ordinary time. You make a joke, you hand me a piece of candy. My mother appears at your side. You speak to her about me and tell her what needs to be done. She keeps glancing at me solicitously. I allow her concern to enter me, but only up to that luminous border within myself, behind which I now exist outside of fear and desire. As you leave, you look at me once again. Silently, I promise you "I will not allow anything to cross this border in myself." And I then give my body over to my mother and her tender ministrations.

Shall I continue with other pictures of what you were like not so long ago? I want you to come back; we all want it; we all dream of it.

I can see you smiling indulgently at me as I write this. But wait, hear me out. I tell you that you yourself have forgotten what you stood for in people's lives. Perhaps you never really knew it—how could you? Like all of us, you are a product of the times. How could you know that your role was one of the very last surviving traces of the sacred in our world? I do not say the "religious"; I say the sacred. Let me explain what I mean.

Do you remember when my grandfather died? You had been treating him for diabetes and heart disease for several years when suddenly his condition began to deteriorate and he had to take to his bed. You loved him probably as much as everyone else. You used to come to our house even without being called, just because of the warmth you felt there from my grandfather and grandmother. I remember one Passover *seder*, when you were our guest and when all my relatives were there and everyone had drunk a great deal of sweet wine. You drank a toast to my grandparents, saying you had never seen such a large family so harmoniously bound to each other.

On the morning of the day he died, after examining him, you quietly took my mother aside and told her to prepare for the worst. In a very short time her sister—my aunt—and all my uncles with their wives rushed to our house and somberly assembled in the living room. My grandmother, who died suddenly only two months later, was with my grandfather and never left his side.

One by one my mother, my aunt, and my uncles each went upstairs to his room and then came down, their eyes wet with tears. I remember that I was sitting next to you on the couch. I did not want to leave your side, not even when my father appeared.

Then the rabbi came, an old man whom I had only seen at the pulpit in the synagogue. He, too, went upstairs and when he came down, he also had tears in his eyes. When I saw that *he* was crying, something broke in me and I began to cry too. I looked over to my father, who had his arm around my mother, comforting her. Then I looked up at you and you turned to me and said, softly, "You have to see him, too, before he dies."

Do you have any idea what those words meant to me? I was five years old and it was my first direct experience with death. I was being torn apart by a maelstrom of emotions, but you made me feel that in the midst of all that, I was under an obligation. It was the first time I ever understood that there is such a thing as objective duty. It made an indelible impact on me. In my childhood, all other shoulds and oughts were imposed upon me from outside and I always—unconsciously, of course—kept my inner self untouched by them, in rebellion against them.

But what you said also sounded from somewhere deep inside me. My whole body was galvanized in effortless obedience as once again that special silence appeared and I was in the world of men, not children. There, inside that border, there was no fear or self- pity, only sorrow and a feeling of strength as I climbed the stairs.

The door to my grandparents' room was open and as I reached the top of the stairs, I looked down the hallway and saw my grandfather lying in his bed, propped up against the pillows. At first I thought he was smiling at me, but when I entered the room, I saw that he was not conscious. His face was ashen and covered with white stubble. The room smelled very bad.

My grandmother, with a big, white shawl around her shoulders, was sitting unmovingly in a chair beside the bed. I went and stood next to her. Time stopped—I felt as though I were in another world, another land, the world where these two people, my grandparents, really came from. I thought of the word *Europe*, which is where my mother had told me they were born. "This must be what 'Europe' is like," I thought. I sensed that they had once existed before my mother was born and therefore a long, long time before I was born. I sensed that there was a time that they lived for each other and not only for us. And now, once again, they existed for each other. Without thinking twice about it, I climbed on the bed and kissed my grandfather's scratchy face. When I climbed down from the bed, I looked at my grandmother. She did not turn her head, but her eyes met mine. I touched her lightly on the shoulder and felt an extraordinary sensation of warmth down the length of my spine.

When I came back down the stairs, I was stunned to see my parents and all my relatives standing around the rabbi with their heads bowed, chanting in Hebrew. What shocked me was the sadness in their voices and especially in the voice of the rabbi. I did not feel sad. On the contrary, I felt an immense and quiet joy and straightness.

That impression, as I slowly came down the stairs, was one of those moments that stand forever engraved in the memory, but which are understood only much later in one's life, if at all. I saw myself being pulled into the sadness of the chanting as a kind of wrong interpretation of my state of being, wrong but powerful and seductive.

But because you were there, it did not happen. You were standing off to the side, respectfully looking on, but without participating. When I came to the bottom of the stairs, I chose to go stand next to you, even though my older cousin, who was now also present and standing beside my aunt, beckoned me. I went and stood next to you and remained there. I was more united to you and my grandparents.

That, dear doctor, is what I mean when I say you represented the sacred. Perhaps you think I have not explained myself well. We shall see, we shall see . . . please be patient with me.

2. A Great and Honorable Passion

I can hear you saying, "Today we might have saved your grandfather's life with bypass surgery or kidney dialysis. He might have lived another five or even ten years!"

But what is that I hear in your voice? It is true, what you say, but why does it sound so hollow when you say it? There was a time, doctor, when your passion to save lives echoed of something beyond death itself! I repeat: Your passion was higher than anything else in our lives. When I watched you close the eyes of my dead grandfather, I felt that I was in the presence of a power of reality that more nearly deserves the name of Man than anything else we know in our ordinary lives. This power is twofold, only one aspect of which had a name. There was death—there in the body of my beloved grandfather. And there was another power as well, equal and opposite to death—there in you, coming through you. What is the opposite of death? It is not what *we* call life, that I know, and I knew it then as a young child. The fact of his death was stronger by far than all the life around him, all the sadness and all the religion. And it was stronger by far than your science and your knowledge. Standing over my grandfather, you also stood in front of death without bending your neck down or up, without surrendering either to earth or heaven. I don't know the name of this passion to understand and to help, which manifests as objectivity in the face of death itself. I don't know its name—that means I don't know where in man it resides. I know only that it is connected to something in ourselves that is equal and opposite to the fact of death.

It was not science you believed in, it was man. But today it is science you believe in and science, great as it is when it is good, is less than man, far less. When science was new to you, you believed in using it—but you were so very careful about it. You were always watching, looking, never taking anything for granted when you used the methods and the instruments of science. You were an observer and your eyes were in your heart as well as your head. You were a good scientist, because you were a man who was always testing science itself.

But now science is no longer new for you. You no longer put it to the test when you act. More important, it no longer puts you to the test. It has swallowed your mind. There is no longer a creative struggle in you between your own intuition and the whole of science. You have intuition, you have your own direct experience, your own hard-earned certainties, but they have all been isolated in some kind of concentration camp of the psyche. No one knows where they are; no one knows they exist; no one believes they are all in prison, starving, dying, tortured.

Somewhere in you, doctor, there exists your own real experience, but you are intimidated and can no longer find your way back to that place in yourself where personal conviction confronts the conventional wisdom. Only in that confrontation between one's own experience and socially accepted knowledge, can there appear the mature observer with his unique, specifically human energy and passion. In that confrontation there is only one thing to trust: attention.

Admit it, you *are* intimidated by science—you who, of all people, witness every day the unpredictability of life. We poor philosophers live amid pristine ideas and arguments, while you are out in the front lines wrestling with real nature. How foolish of you to rely so much on our concepts and ideas that were created in a vacuum of isolated thought. What? You mean you didn't know that the methods and concepts of modern science were created by bored philosophers?

Forgive me. I'm getting carried away. I'm overstating things. It's only that I see your passion has drifted away from your science. And so I'm forced again to ask myself: Why do I care so much for you? You're no different from everyone else—you, too, like everyone else, have lost hold of the meaning of your life and work. Like all of us, your passions are only weaknesses, not strengths. Still, yours *was* the last as well as the first great and honorable passion of man—the fusion of two loves, the love of knowledge and the love of man, the fusion of the search for understanding and the impulse to help and serve suffering humanity. I'm sorry, but that *is* what you represent to me, to us. What you once represented.

Call it a myth, if you like, a dream, a mere ideal. But, admit it, doesn't something sound in you—perhaps from afar—when you are reminded of this ideal? "I am busy," you say. "I have much to do, real needs to meet as best I can. There are urgent things to be done, difficult decisions to be made. There is not enough time, people need my immediate help. I do what I can, I take what works . . . "

Yes, doctor, yes. You are obliged. Your role cannot be dispensed with in any civilization. It has always existed; it will always exist. You are necessary. But I tell you, your obligations weigh you down and defeat you because you are cut off from the metaphysical reality of your role in human life. You can't waste time on mere ideals, yet it is ideals that create time. Time, doctor, is energy. Your ideals no longer bring you energy because you no longer feel them. And so, you have abandoned your ideals as distractions—or, what is worse—you have tamed them into elegant, ethical pets that you sport with in your precious "free time."

Do you think I am writing to castigate you? I am not, believe me. I am writing to you because I need your *look*, your power to *see*, which you have squandered. Science, doctor, is *seeing*. That is how our science was born—long, long ago in remote antiquity. In the shadows of the great Pythagoras. We must speak about that some time. Did you know that the oath of Hippocrates is a document of the Pythagoreans? We must speak about it; it will intrigue you to realize that empirical medicine, medicine based on the revolutionary act of looking attentively at what is right before one's eyes, springs from the greatest mystical teachings. It will intrigue you to realize that faithfulness to the visible world springs from faithfulness to the invisible world.

However, that is not the point. The point is passion, the passion of an authentic man seeking to inhabit his authentic place in the whole great scheme of reality. Science inevitably must arise out of that passion and only out of that passion. Listen: Medicine is the first science of civilization. It was so in China; it was so in Egypt; it is so in all times and all cultures. Impartial observation exists only as a result of the fusion of two loves—for my own being and for the well-being of my neighbor.

This fact is something about us, about human nature, that is not in our philosophy; or should I say it is only in our philosophy, only in our heads. But you, doctor, once lived it—if only to a degree and unconsciously. Man is a giving being. This defines our nature more than anything else. Our need is to give; we are built to give. All that we receive is to this end. Everything that is wrong with us is because this is not understood. We are constructed to serve.

At the same time, man has nothing to give. He is weak, helpless, suffocated by ego and the fear of death. You are constructed for service to Being yet you are ruled by a dying animal living in fantastic dreams. Science was born in the direct experience of this contradiction in human nature—it was born as medicine.

3. We Who Are About to Die

Are you still with me? Or have I gone too far speaking about things that have no direct bearing on your work?

But what is your work? No, don't dismiss this question too quickly. It is not a rhetorical question. What is your work? And why is this such a difficult question to answer?

Is it because there is really no such thing as being *purely* practical? You are impatient with pure idealism, mere idealism that is not effective in action. And yours is a calling to action, to heal, to relieve suffering. But I say that man was not meant to be purely practical. You, doctor, just you will die in your tracks if you go on seeking to be purely practical. You are dying in your tracks, and you know it. Just as those of us who have tried to live by mind alone long ago died in our tracks. Man is not a pure being. And none of his real undertakings can be pure—that is to say, single, one-natured. Man is two-fold.

You know, you yourself first taught me this. I'm sure you don't remember, but it was when I was twelve years old. There was something wrong with me that you weren't able to diagnose and you sent me for tests and X rays at the University of Pennsylvania clinic where you also worked one afternoon each week.

The large receiving room was jammed with hundreds of people sitting on benches waiting to be called. I leaned against a wall next to a hissing radiator and took out one of my schoolbooks. An hour passed, then another. Finally, I put my book away and began just to watch the people coming and going.

My attention was caught first by an old man shuffling past me. His clothes were ragged and he had a huge, protuberant belly that burst through the buttons of his pants. He was unshaven. Mucus dripped from his nose. I quickly turned my eyes from him, but as I did so I noticed that his gray-black hair was carefully combed and neatly parted in the middle. There flashed before my mind the image of this ugly old man, suffering from God knows what illness, standing in front of his bathroom mirror painstakingly parting his hair. This man, to my mind, was as good as dead, yet he worried about parting his hair!

I looked toward the entrance doors and saw a young black man, with sullen, striking good looks, ambling down the side aisle. He was practically strutting, lord of all he surveyed, graceful and menacing at the same time, wearing a purple jacket and brilliant, sharply creased crimson slacks. Look out for that man! Step aside! Yet right under it all, he too was only a sick body that needed help and knowledge. How pathetic and even poignant his plumage seemed to me.

And what of that young woman sitting in the second row of benches reading her copy of *The New Yorker*? What is that flesh-colored pouch resting on the bench next to her with a tube discreetly leading under her bright yellow jacket? Isn't that for draining the excreta from her intestines? Why flesh-colored? This young woman, with her sweet blond hair and pretty lips—wasn't she herself only a flesh-colored pouch? Didn't she know that? *I* knew it.

Or that hawk-faced, white-haired man in a dark suit and subtly patterned maroon tie, his legs elegantly crossed, his arms folded tightly across his chest, looking for all the world like some transplanted Nordic king before whom one bends the knee in fear and awe—what is that swelling on his neck? What disease is growing beneath the facade of power and strength? Human man in a human body.

Impressions of human mortality began shouting at me through every man, woman and child in the room. I saw in all of them so many heartbreakingly transparent attempts to paint over their own fragility. They seemed to me like broken toys still whirring and spinning just before they stopped. That Oriental woman wearing a neck brace and in her hair a gardenia! Those two lovers holding hands and gazing at each other—he with half his face covered by a thick bandage! That frighteningly thin black woman, looking like a living skeleton, dressed in orange lace. That obese boy, no older than I, wearing a tautly stretched sweatshirt with the insignia of a football team on it—his chest rapidly moving up and down as though even sitting quietly he could not take in enough air for his monstrous bulk. That aging woman with rings on all her fingers checking her makeup in a little mirror, her face white as paper under the thick smudges of rouge.

Do you know it was then that I decided to become a doctor? Some people say that they went into medicine in order to help their fellow man. But I think that is not exactly true, even for the most idealistic people. For me, in any case, my desire to become a doctor was based on the perception that there was *nothing* that could possibly help my fellow man. I saw that everyone was condemned to death, and quite soon at that. I saw that the people, the little egos, existed like blown leaves floating meaninglessly on an ocean of death, and this ocean of death was the great universe itself in all its beauty and order. Doctor, doctor, do you see what I mean? I felt *truth* in that perception! What matter that the truth was terrifying? It was the truth, it was truth! And it opened in my breast such a flood of compassion as I have rarely experienced since in my life. It was truth that brought compassion, that awakened in myself a higher power of feeling, of love.

And yet these people needed help. They needed to live, to be healed, to be cured. They needed to live a tiny bit longer, with a tiny bit less pain, less suffering, less fear. They could not be helped, yet they need to be helped and they could be helped—a little, an immense little.

Don't recoil at this contradiction. It is not a logical contradiction that people are as good as dead, yet need to live. It is a metaphysical contradiction that defines human nature itself. You taught me that—*you*. Then, that very afternoon. I watched you working at your office in the clinic. Do you remember? After I left the X-ray room, I came to your corner of the clinic. The door of the examining room was open and seated on the table was that fat old man with the neatly parted hair. He was naked except for a sheet draped over his thighs, and his monstrous white abdomen hung down nearly to his knees. You were seated on a stool between his dangling legs with one arm embracing him and with the side of your face pressed against his chest. In your other hand you clutched your stethoscope, which you had obviously abandoned in favor of listening to the man's chest directly with your ear.

Something like a current of electricity passed through me when I saw that. Your eyes met mine as I passed by, but you didn't acknowledge me. I didn't exist for you at that moment. I smiled nervously at you, but nothing came from you toward me. You were with that fat old man, not me.

I swung past the door again, hoping you would smile at me. Nothing of the kind. Once again, you looked through me as though I didn't exist. Doctor, I have seen your colleagues—many, many of them—show to their patients agreeable emotions that— forgive my crude language—are as shit compared to what I sensed in you in those days. And I have seen their coldness and indifference, their "importance," their "busyness"; I've seen them all overburdened, their attention scattered or driven back by fear. But what was in you was not coldness, not indifference, not busyness. Although my feelings were hurt for a moment, deep down I understood in my heart that your concern to help was a completely different level of feeling and love. You were not out to "please" anyone. You were not concerned with "the relationship to the patient," as they put it nowadays. And I, as a patient, felt that and it gave me more strength and more trust in you than you can possibly imagine.

It was not the power of science that I trusted in you. You make a mistake when you think that. People don't trust science; people trust people. They don't trust religion; they trust people. They don't trust psychiatry or schools; they trust people. Similarly, people don't distrust medicine or science, or religion or politics; they distrust doctors, scientists, priests, psychiatrists, politicians; they distrust people. And why? What is the key to all this? The key is nonegoistic, impersonal love. The key is the metaphysical contradiction of impersonal love. You cared for that old man as much as you cared for me. Yet you were a friend of my family; you tousled my hair, you gave me candy, you called me by amusing names. But then and there you cared for that old man more than you cared for me. And to sense that sent chills of a strange, subtle joy up my spine.

How to put it? You loved that man's existence, his life. That means: You loved the fact of life itself, the fact of nature, creation, and order. You weren't just interested; you loved. And you acted to preserve life; you actually did things with your time and your hands, things that worked, that made a material difference in the material world. You acted, as they say in the world of ideas, in *history*, in human affairs. You loved. You were more than a priest sowing dreams of a better world; more than a therapist dispensing pleasant emotions to an ego with neatly parted hair. This, doctor, is a metaphysical contradiction. You were not pure. And we are not pure. We are existence, life, nature that goes on forever in the eternity of universal law; *and* we are little unreal selves who are about to die. In front of death and the mortal body, you cared for life. I don't know what that means. I don't know the ultimate resolution of that contradiction, and you did not know it either. But it must exist.

Your action, the role you occupy in human life is tangible proof that the resolution of this contradiction does exist. For consider: Either you are performing an absurd, though kindly, service to us—tending our bodies on their wobbling little way to annihilation—or else you are giving us time to penetrate some mystery that reality itself demands of us. Either you are helping us to become more comfortable sheep or you are helping us to become men. There is no in-between. There is no middle ground. Artists, geniuses, scientists, statesmen—we are all either sheep or real men; that is, on the way to being either dead sheep or living individual representatives of Great Being. The body tells us that, reminds us of that, *is* that possibility and that contradiction. Do what you will, dress as you will, part your hair ever so neatly—still, your belly hangs down to your knees just before you descend into the earth. Your physical body, our physical body, is the sound of law and necessity beyond all our big thoughts, egoistic passions, "great discoveries." In this purely physical realm, even we can recognize that we live in a universe of unbending law. And I say that this world of unbending law has two movements in it, two directions, two possibilities—one toward inner growth and the other toward dissolution. In the way *you* love and care for us and our bodies—in just that way we will tend to orient ourselves toward being, necessity, universal law—the cosmos. Call it God, I don't care. I don't need that word. Do you?

My name is called and I go into the examining room to wait for you. The nurse is attaching my X rays, still wet from the developer, to the lightframe. After she leaves, I stare at the ghostly bones of my feet for a few minutes. Then I hear your voice outside and I quickly scramble to my place on the table.

I hear another voice, too, sharply interrupting you and suddenly a short man with a narrow, pink face and closely cropped gray hair bursts into the room, his unbuttoned white coat billowing out to the sides like a royal cape as he hurries past me. You follow him, nervously.

Yes, nervously. Something wakes up in me. What is going on? Who is this thin little man with all this concentrated power to whom *you* defer? Who in the world is higher than you?

I am astonished by the way you listen to him as he points his finger to a certain precise place on the X rays, where the Achilles tendon joins the heel. His speech is crisp, rapid and sure, just like his gestures and movements.

Let me break off this narrative for a moment. I want to say something as clearly and distinctly as possible. Bear in mind this *tableau*: I am twelve years old, seated on the examining table. I have been experiencing pain in my feet, the remotest corners of my body, so I am not yet very afraid of anything. I have only just resolved to become a doctor myself, having felt in one stroke—very powerfully—the contradiction between the fragility of man and the greatness of nature, together with the mystery of your dedication. Somehow, in the way you cared for these pathetic

human beings I sensed an inexplicable bridge between the universe and our little selves. I sensed that if I could do what you
do, I could become a conscious part of the whole greatness of
nature itself.

I know you have half-jokingly told me that you went into
medicine because you wanted to be "on the winning side—
because it's the patient, not the doctor, who dies." But of course
this way of putting it—that you became a physician because you
feared death—is a corruption, a caricature of the feeling that I
am speaking of and that I know lies behind your own passion,
your former passion. Your love was not absurd, was not an
existentialist posture—absurd man acting morally in an indiffer-
ent universe. Your passion was itself a fragment of something
that comes from another level in the universe; tangible proof that
there are other forces in the cosmos than those that we can
measure by our senses or our instruments. Let me give a name
to what it evoked in me—what its roots are in you. I call it *moral
wonder*.

By the word *wonder,* I intend something quite precise. It is the
same intuitive certainty that appears when, in very special moments, I look at the sky full of stars or at the workings of nature
in a living creature or single cell—the felt certainty that I am in
front of a reality immeasurably greater in *kind* than I am. Such
experiences of wonder, however, may lack one thing—the certainty that this immeasurably greater reality is concerned about
me—just me, this pathetic little ego that I know myself to be.
Nor do these moments guide me, irresistibly and joyously, to care
for my neighbor as being also a particle of the great wholeness
of nature. That's why I call the feeling that your dedication
evoked in me moral wonder. It is like looking at the stars and
knowing that they are looking back at me.

I have never felt this in front of the other sorts of actions that
the world calls moral or ethical. I have never felt that the passion
of other sorts of well-intentioned people was a force of nature,
part of the real world, directed to the real in man, involved in
the bedrock laws and forces of the bedrock universe itself. Only

in your passion have I seen—may I say it this way?—"proof" of the existence of God. Other acts of moral concern have somehow always left me suspicious, even bored or frightened. Not to put too fine a point on it: I have always smelled something egoistic, invented, sentimental, or futile and naive in all these other moralities that are so enthusiastically prized in our society.

This *tableau*, then: Twelve year old. Sitting on the examination table. Seeing you, the hero of my childhood, the sun—so to say—of my cosmos, obediently listening to this intense little man, taking instruction from him! I felt: He is to you as you are to me! Levels. Levels, doctor. Of knowledge and wisdom and love. In the world of men as in the universe itself!

Are you smiling at me again? Don't. Don't tell me that this orthopedic specialist was only a tense and arrogant little man who just happened to be, as they say nowadays, "charismatic." I know all that. I know about these imposing personages of previous generations around whom legends formed—professors of medicine, heads of departments, famous specialists. I know about their vanity and weaknesses. Yet these teachers of medicine were the nearest thing our modern culture has ever had to the spiritual guide. They were tyrants, I know that. We badly need such tyrants to come back.

They made impossible demands. Impossible yet possible. They embodied the demands of nature itself. How can you meet real nature, the real forces of life, with the socially acceptable level of feeling? You cannot. No one can. The laws of life and death cannot be confronted with our weak wills made up, as they are, by a chaotic parade of compulsions and attractions. These tyrants demanded dedication, service to truth. Medicine can never be taught only intellectually. Medicine is not science in that sense. Or rather, it is real science—science rooted in the mind of the heart. You will agree, doctor, that intelligence appears only when there is urgency. Need. When we are so trapped by the problem before us that we have no choice but to become still. Only then does the movement toward myself appear and only then does my real, original mind begin to speak.

They demanded total dedication and you responded with total dedication. I know all about the mixture of vanity, fear, and ego that was part of their nature. They had big egos, granted. But they served something bigger than the ego and you felt that! They made you do without sleep, without money, without sex—like some burning monk seeking God. They made you give your attention to the big picture—the welfare of the patient—as well as to the tiniest technical detail, like some burning monk copying a sacred book. They rubbed your nose in your incapacities while demanding that you take it all with a quiet mind, a mind free of panic and self-love. They made you feel your responsibility—you were a doctor, after all—while demeaning you in front of the real level of ability that was their standard of excellence. They forced you into that sacred place in between what you are and what you can become.

I call that education.

In any case, it is not "pragmatic." It is not merely "useful," "workable." Or should I say, rather, that this approach to the art of medicine is nearer to the pragmatism of nature itself, the human body itself. In the body there are many creatures—plants, animals, songbirds, devils and angels, and machines. Some push and pull, some run wildly after their food and sex, some raise their eyes to heaven and do nothing but sing, some spin and whir according to mechanical law. In the sacred pragmatism of the whole of nature, all these creatures coexist in all their contradictions. You cannot meet the human organism when you yourself ride only one of them. You have to ride them all. You have to occupy the place of instinct, the animal forces of biological nature; you have to occupy the gardens of feeling and tenderness and sweet intuition where the language of the birds is spoken; you have to sit within the engines and machinery of the purely physical objects. You have to know when to pull levers, when to croon, when to shout, when to strike and kill, when to merely watch and wait, when to embrace, when to cut and separate— and all through the flesh and bones and guts you can see before you. And you have to think, reason, prove—when necessary. The power to do all that does not come from studying books, or from laboratory experiments alone, nor even from working with patients under the protective umbrella of professionalism and advanced technology.

All of that, and much more, is what that twelve-year-old boy felt sitting on the examination table. Not in words, of course. But when that slender god left the room as brusquely as he came in, you remained for a long time staring at the X rays. I knew exactly what had happened. That little god had corrected you in no uncertain terms. He had not spared your feelings, even with me present in the room. And here is the strange thing: This increased my awe of you! I could not understand to what you were obedient. It was not to that little man, I knew that. I sensed your human qualities and knew they were greater than those of that other doctor—after all, I knew you from childhood; I knew your kindness and impartiality; nothing could shake that knowledge. But what was this *greater* that you obeyed and deferred to? I wanted to obey it too.

Finally, you turned toward me and sat down on the low stool in front of me. You took off my shoes and socks and grasped my foot in your hand. With your other hand you touched my ankle and the back of my heel. You slowly pushed my foot upward, stretching the Achilles tendon. "Let me know exactly when this begins to hurt."

And so on. In a very short time, you were standing up, telling me to put my shoes back on.

When you told me that for six months I would need to have both my legs in casts, I simply nodded. Suddenly, everything became silent in me. I wanted to obey something, something bigger than myself, but all I could feel was fear rising up within me, making me so intensely silent. So this was what it was like to actually be part of nature, reality.

You didn't make pleasantries, you didn't even explain what was wrong with me. (I learned later that the tendons had separated from the heel; the specialist had recommended surgery; you chose otherwise.)

You gave me a pair of crutches and told me to practice with them before coming to your office the following day to have the casts put on.

Why didn't you say anything more? And if there was nothing to say, why did you not simply dismiss me from the room? There were so many other patients waiting, old people, people much sicker than I. Why did you simply allow me to sit on that table while you briskly went about some business or other in the room, shuffling charts, taking down my X rays, washing your hands? I know what was happening in me—did you know it, too? Did you sense it? I was finding my own strength. I believe you sensed that. My own strength.

Eventually, I slid down from the table and walked out of the examining room, crutches in hand. I felt empty, and alive.

"See you tomorrow," you said.

I turned to look at you. Your eyes did not give an inch. All they did was to confirm my state of inner presence.

4. Impressions

I still have the letter I wrote to you, and never mailed, around the time I decided not to become a doctor. You probably remember the events surrounding that modest little tempest, especially the Napoleonic campaign waged by my parents to get me to change my mind. You certainly remember the meeting you had with me, for their sake. Your "assignment" was to persuade me to go to medical school. But when you saw the emotional state I was in, you didn't force the issue. Considering how strangely I behaved in your office that winter afternoon, I suppose you really had no choice. Your forbearance was commendable.

And yet, because you didn't command me to go on, the heart went out of me. You said I had to discover what I really wanted, that I should not let anyone compel me. You did the "right" thing with me. But the "right" thing was wrong. The "wrong" thing was what I craved from you. Unconsciously, I needed you to remind me, in no uncertain terms, of the sacredness of medicine.

Will you allow me now, nearly thirty years later, to explain what was going on in me? I can think of no better way to illustrate all that I am trying to say to you now about the meaning of the practice of medicine.

At the beginning of my second year of college, I took a part-time job as an orderly at the Cambridge General Hospital, a few blocks away from the university campus. Like many city hospitals, it was run on inadequate funds and served mainly emergency cases and indigents (government medical insurance did not yet exist). Because of the low budget, it was actually a more interesting place to work; employees like me were given a variety of jobs that otherwise would have been divided among more specialized personnel. I was assigned to the men's postoperative recovery ward where my duties comprised those of a physician's assistant, nurse's aide, and janitor. Most of the patients were elderly derelicts.

I also served as a very original kind of messenger boy, ferrying large and small pieces of the the human body from the operating room to the pathology laboratory. This required a strong stomach. At any given time, I might be called to the operating room where I would be handed anything from a piece of tissue in a petri dish to a whole human leg or arm, which I had to wrap in newspaper and carry through the halls and elevators to another wing of the building.

Fortunately, I had worked during the previous summer as an autopsy assistant at the University of Pennsylvania hospital and had no difficulty with the more grisly aspects of this task. That experience in the autopsy room was extraordinary in many ways, as it happened to be a very "busy" summer and I had to help with two or three corpses every day. My "customers" included children and young men and women along with the aged. My job was to scrub down the bodies and, after the autopsy, to dispose of the internal organs and to stuff the visceral cavity with excelsior. I also had to saw open the skull in a very exact way, remove the brain for sectioning, tie off the major cranial blood vessels and then replace the skull and sew up the entire body for delivery to the funeral parlor.

As you may well imagine, that summer produced many powerful impressions. But looking back on it now, and in the light of the experience I was soon to have at Cambridge General, two things stand out, both connected with this whole question of having "a strong stomach." I hope I can communicate to you why this is of such interest to me and why I think it is of such importance. I have not seen or heard it spoken of anywhere and I very much want to have your views on it. It has to do with including the physical-instinctive side of the psyche in one's development as a human being and as a physician.

There were two aspects of my work in the autopsy room that I never grew accustomed to: sawing open the skull and incinerating the viscera. In both cases, the smell violently affected me. The dust of the skull always penetrated the surgical mask I wore and brought me to the point of nausea. It was an indescribably acrid stench. The burning viscera, on the other hand, gave off an aroma, even through the sealed metal door of the incinerator, that was very much like that of food being cooked. What disturbed me in the latter case was the simultaneous presence in me of two contradictory reactions: an emotional aversion toward the fact that these were the viscera of human beings, and an instinctual savoring of the aroma they gave off when they were burning. As for the other case, there, too, I was in between contradictory impulses—one of instinctual aversion toward the stench of the dust and the other a passionate interest, which never failed to appear, in the wonder of the human brain.

I was troubled and also bemused by the great spectrum of reactions evoked in me during this period and could not understand the calm and ease with which the doctors—whom I assisted during the autopsy—treated everything. At first, I assumed that they had learned to master such reactions and I respected their objectivity and concentration. But by the end of summer, my respect for the doctors had dimmed without my knowing exactly why. I had a gnawing sense that their apparent objectivity was really a kind of numbness.

In the excitement of the beginning of the school year, all these impressions moved to the background, but they came to the fore again when I assumed my duties as an orderly.

It began on the very first day of my job with an incident that still makes me laugh and shudder when I think back on it. While I was being acquainted with all the tasks that I would have to perform on the ward, a call came from the OR that a specimen had to be delivered to pathology, and I was sent to do the errand. Dressed in my crisp hospital whites, I hurried to the OR and introduced myself as the new surgical orderly. Matter-of-factly, the attendant handed me a large, stainless-steel basin containing a human leg that had been amputated just below the knee. I did not blink an eye, but when I was on the other side of the doors,

I propped myself against the wall until my head stopped swimming. Two very vivid thoughts came to my mind and stayed there: I thought with sadness of the young woman whose leg this was and, at the same time I thought, as I looked closely at the leg, that if in the entire universe nothing else had existed except this extraordinary object, even then God the Creator would deserve to be worshipped.

Following instructions, I wrapped the leg in newspaper and marched into the corridor with this remarkable package tucked firmly under my arm. Not knowing my way about the hospital, however, I found myself walking through areas crowded with visitors and began to worry that some nonmedical person would see what I was carrying and would faint there on the spot. Surreptitiously, I adjusted the newspaper so that it would not have the shape of the object it contained. I was disturbed to see that the paper was already soaked with blood—I had neglected to wrap the leg first in a sheet of plastic.

Unable to locate the service elevators, I nervously entered one of the public elevators that, on the next stop, suddenly became so crowded with all sorts of people that it almost burst. When I saw that blood was now dripping from the package, I clumsily tried to double the loose papers at the bottom. At just that moment, the doors opened again and a fat woman standing behind me charged through the crowd to get out, knocking against me in the process. The package flew out of my arms and, as the doors closed, there for all to see was a bloody human leg reposing on the floor.

There were screams, shouts of "Oh, my God!" and an extraordinary amount of physical movement, considering the narrow, enclosed space of the elevator.

In moments such as this, one becomes acutely and quietly aware of all the contradictory impulses in oneself. In the brief time that passed before the doors opened on the next floor and the occupants of the elevator rushed out in a mad dash, I witnessed several things in myself, as though my consciousness were looking down from the ceiling in Olympian impartiality.

My first impulse was to pretend it was not my fault and to act as shocked as eveyone else, which I did so persuasively that, even with my blood-soaked clothes, the passengers did not see me— until the next impulse manifested itself, even more absurd than the first. I heard myself apologizing in tones appropriate to some-one who has dropped a teacup at a dinner party—"I beg your pardon, please excuse me"—and when I bent down to pick up the object it produced a new and even louder round of shrieks and agitation. All the while, from far down in myself, a huge wave of laughter was rising and, alongside it, a sensation of absolute terror and disgust in the pit of my stomach. It seems that for a brief instant, as I bent over to pick up the severed leg, my eyes fell on all the other human legs that were crowded around me; and right there, in the pit of my stomach, I experi-enced an instinctual comprehension of the mortal destiny of all the individual human bodies in that elevator that were attached to those legs.

As I look back on it now, I see that this incident was the psychological trigger of the crisis that built up in me during the three months that followed. Because of this incident, my experi-ences on the surgical ward attained an unusual intensity and balance for someone as immature as I was, involving not only emotional reactions but also perceptions of human suffering that reached down, however slightly, to my instinctual mind as well.

All the memories of my summer in the autopsy room returned in full force and stayed with me the whole time I worked at Cambridge General in the postoperative recovery room. In addi-tion to running bedpans, changing dirty sheets, and sweeping up, I was obliged to give alcohol baths to all the patients, to help them eat, to clean up their vomit, and to wipe their asses. I fed them, washed them, and tucked them in and as they recovered, I helped them dress and walk around. In addition, I was instructed in techniques of penile catheterization, a procedure that was re-quired for every patient. It always amazed me that what seemed such a thick, coarse tube could be quite simply and easily inserted into the most delicate and modest of a man's bodily orifices. But

I soon learned not only that every natural opening in the human body is a channel for substances passing in and out but that the whole human body, every square inch of it, is an orifice. I began to understand, also, that this body is a machine made up of tubes, wires, pumps, filters, batteries, sounding boards, cushions, support beams, casings, and so on. Emotionally and intellectually, this was all extremely interesting in both a positive and negative sense—but what I am trying to say is that these experiences were being received down deep somewhere in my own body, in my own instinctual mind. And what this meant, as I now understand it and as I wish you to understand it, became clear when, only three days after I had started on the ward, one of the patients—an old man named Patterson—died in my arms.

Before telling you about this, however, I should say that during the present year I have been giving lectures and workshops to various groups of physicians on the general subject of "human values in the practice of medicine." This has given me the chance to interview many doctors on a very personal, individual basis and to ask them the kind of questions that no one ever asks them directly in this period of our civilization. One of the questions I have asked—and at first I did so with great trepidation and modesty—is quite simply: "Have you ever seen a human being die?" By that question, I did not mean having a patient who died, or being present right before and after death. My question concerned the actual process of passing from life to the state of death. I was asking the doctors if they had ever watched that happen.

I naturally expected that they would all answer "of course, countless times" and perhaps regard me—a mere layman—with some degree of condescension for understandably making a great deal out of an experience that in their profession takes place as part of their everyday work. But to my amazement, most of them answered *no*, either directly or indirectly (that is, scratching their heads, thinking for a few minutes, and then nonchalantly saying yes after dimly locating the occasion in their memory somewhere).

And this, doctor, is why I am emboldened to tell you in detail about this death I witnessed when I was a hospital orderly nearly thirty years ago. There are impressions, experiences that, by their nature, act upon a human being to raise the deepest kind of questions, the deepest sense of wonder and shock, that touch the eternal energy locked in the human mind—experiences which are like, and even stronger than, great ideas that come from a higher level of mind, awakening and supporting the wish for truth and being—experiences that call forth the transcendent in man in the form of a yearning presence. The vocation of medicine by its very nature is given to contain more of such experiences than perhaps any other profession of contemporary life. Yet modern medicine offers fewer and fewer of them—in this case due, partly, to the advance of modern technology that has blurred the clarity of death. Death has not been in the slightest degree overcome by a modern technology that maintains the bodily functions long after the animating principle of a human being has disintegrated. But the clarity of this moment of irreversible disintegration has become clouded over by the technical ability to maintain one or another of the component aspects of this animating principle. As a result, there is now a desperate and futile quest for a "definition of death," that is to say, for an intellectual definition of death. However, death cannot be defined intellectually—it can only be intuited. The mirage of an intellectual definition of death obscures its organic decisiveness, just as in my own field, mere intellectual definitions of great ideas obscure the vital rational meaning of great truths about man and the universal order.

It was during the second week of my employment at the hospital, when I had already grown quite accustomed to certain aspects of the routine there. John Patterson was an elderly, retired longshoreman of very slight stature, with a leathery, toothless face and a long, hooked nose that gave him a lightly comical, Punch-and-Judy expression. He was what is considered a "difficult" patient, though far from being that kind of intractable, half-demented creation of contemporary technology known derisively as a *gomer*—that is, a two-thirds dead, biologically alive wonder of science who never gets better or worse and who, or which, is impervious to both compassion and hostility on the part of the frustrated, guilt-ridden residents who are responsible for his care.

Mr. Patterson had undergone surgery for a bleeding duodenal ulcer and began coming out of anesthesia while I was in the process of catheterizing him. My first acquaintance with him found me on the receiving end of a mumbled, semiconscious, but virulently vulgar imprecation based on his dazed perception of my relationship to his penis—something on the order of "Get your hands off my cock, you fuckin' faggot!"

As you can well imagine, these words went through me like a lightning bolt and a strong feeling of hatred for this old, ungrateful, and disgusting man flared up in me just at the moment that I was dealing directly, with my own hands, with several of his bodily fluids and orifices. But when I looked up at him and saw his toothless, comical old face, I happened to remember what he had just been through and for some reason the other two impulses in me—physical distaste and emotional hatred—fused together with what I knew in my mind about his prognosis, which was very bad as he had many complications. The result was that I experienced an all-encompassing sensation of compassion for him, completely without emotional agitation.

During the next three days whenever I saw him, this sensation of compassion returned, especially when I was attending to his bodily needs—even though, or perhaps especially because, he continued to insult me. He died on the fourth day just as I was propping up his head in order to try to give him some oatmeal, his first feeding by mouth since the surgery. The oatmeal was dribbling down his chin and he was looking at me—as usual uttering some curse at me. The light simply and suddenly went out of his eyes.

What I am trying to say, doctor—although I realize I am not saying it very well—is that this impression of another man's death entered into me in such a quiet and balanced way that I began from that moment on to regard everything that took place in the hospital from a completely new perspective. Of course, although I can to a certain extent articulate this perspective to you now, I did not have the language or the understanding to do so then. On the contrary, I was young and inexperienced, and had in my mind only a potpourri of modern psychological and philosophical concepts that, besides adding up to no coherent whole, had no relationship to my acquired store of habitual emotional postures. I therefore plunged into a maelstrom of violent emotional reactions to what routinely took place in the hospital all around me.

For example, my experience with Mr. Patterson proved to me beyond a shadow of a doubt that the problem of death had not been touched by all the religious, scientific, and philosophical teachings with which I was acquainted. I understood that this mystery was far, far closer to myself than I had ever imagined and yet at the same time that the answer to it lay in a completely different direction than anyone knew. I understood that death was the only certain penetration of another dimension into the world we human beings live in. Death was proof that another reality existed, a real reality of forces and laws alien to the world we knew.

But I did not even try to speak about this to others. I saw only doctors solving problems, nurses carrying out orders and trying to give emotional support to the patients, and orderlies like myself doing much of the dirty work. When there was death or great suffering on the ward—as there was every day—the response was either businesslike acceptance or, sometimes, emotional reactions (when someone young or particularly interesting died), or occasionally puzzlement. I soon found it all intolerable, young and inexperienced as I was. Every day the world of real reality was announcing its existence on the ward and people behaved as though this world did not exist, as though this world were not constantly pressing in upon us, insisting, demanding that we acknowledge it. I don't want to use the word *God*, but if I had to speak in religious language, I would say that every day God was thrusting his hands and legs into the ward and everyone was simply walking around them, taking no notice. By God, of course, I mean not simply the all-powerful creator but, rather, the earthshaker, the God of Job.

A huge question, like a palpable material force, like a dense cloud, settled into the ward, and people walked through it as though it didn't exist. But it did exist.

Now let me tell you how I have come to understand all this.

Like everything else in the modern world, the practice of medicine has come increasingly under the sway of mechanization, fragmentation, and specialization. So much is a cliche, obvious. Procedures that once required careful attention can now be done in their outer form by machines or by separate, specialized professionals. This has resulted in great progress in medical mechanics, but at the price of a rapid deterioration of the individual medical mind.

I saw that the medical mind requires a harmonic balance of thought, feeling, and instinct. This balance of three factors in the mind of man is what results in medical virtue, which of course is one expression of human virtue as such, or moral power. Out of the blend of thought, feeling, and instinct there arises authentic intuition, courage, and will, all of which, taken together, may be given the ancient name *intelligence*, a word used to great effect by the great Pythagoras and his follower Socrates, and traces of which may be discerned in one or two places in the surviving medical writings of the ancient Greeks.

Today, however, the physician is obliged only to think and decide, the nurse is obliged only to feel and clean up, and the intern is often obliged only to monitor and perform day-to-day procedures.

The physician thinks without feeling or sensing. It is all arranged that way. This is called objectivity. But it is not objectivity, not impartiality. Such thinking reflects only mechanics, only one part of the external world—because it comes from only one part of the human mind. The organic, vital structure of reality is invisible to the merely logical mind. Merely logical thought can be, and now is, duplicated by machines, computers.

It is not that the physician does not have emotions. He may

have plenty of emotions, but they are not and cannot be related to his thought. They simply blow him away. Doctors are quite as human as anyone else. They sometimes cry, they suffer, they grieve; they feel triumph, elation, satisfaction, although perhaps less of these latter pleasant emotions as time and progress march on, and as advanced technology begins to blur the clarity of life and death, health and illness. But all these emotions bring him no knowledge. They are not perceptions. They are only reactions.

The perception of death, and therefore the entire meaning of the calling of medicine, is not possible solely through the logical mind. Nor through the emotional reactions, nor through instinct and the senses. No, death can be known, that is, perceived, only to the extent that these three separate centers of perception work in harmony. This is because death is something that occurs to the whole of a man; therefore, only the whole of the mind can know it.

Thought, by itself, can record and classify it. Emotion, by itself, can hate it or fear it. The senses, by themselves, can only experience its existence.

The physician of today is only one-third of a physician, and he can perceive only one-third of death and life.

But, doctor, here is the point. There are experiences in every human life that act upon us to bring these three centers of perception momentarily closer together. These are the real peak experiences of human life—not those so-called by New Age people. The experience of my neighbor's death is chief among these experiences, but the organization of contemporary medicine prevents these awakening experiences.

Such experiences are no mere metaphysical luxury. No mere philosophical indulgence. They are necessary for the activation of medical intelligence, the power to see the truth about the individual human body itself, about patients, their needs, their actual illnesses, their actual diagnoses and treatment. These experiences are in the practice of medicine exactly what the experience of wonder is in the life of the research scientist. If it could be proved that the conditions of modern science are such that the experience of wonder were prevented from happening, you would agree that such a state of affairs would foreshadow the destruction of science itself. For medicine, for physicians, the experience of death is as necessary as the experience of wonder is for the scientist. In fact, this is what makes the calling of the physician so high, higher even than that of science, more than that of science. Physicians are also scientists—that is, they need to drink from the sense of wonder; but, their calling demands also the confrontation with death. Only these two truly peak experiences—or, as we may more accurately call them, shocks to the personality—can bring him the intelligence and compassion he craves, but which he has nowadays all but given up hope of finding.

This situation, by the way, explains why the practice of medicine has become increasingly drained of real meaning and satisfaction at the present time. I am speaking, of course, about individuals who enter the field of medicine and stay in it because of a motivation that they themselves cannot name. Call it anything you like—the love of truth, the craving to understand life and death, the need to live in the real world, the wish to serve mankind. It is the motivation I always sensed in you, my beloved doctor. But I have learned that this motivation is nourished by two things and only by two things—great ideas and awakening experiences. Imprisoned in the narrow conceptual assumptions of the modern scientific world view (which is scientism, rather than science), medicine has cut itself off from great ideas. And now, in our time, the organization of medical practice, imprisoned in the organization of modern society, has cut medicine off from awakening experiences. Without these two sources of nourishment, efforts to alleviate human suffering and gain knowledge of life turn round and round in ever-narrowing circles.

But now I am once again running ahead of myself. There will be time for us to draw conclusions about how to correct things before the vocation of the physician utterly disappears from our culture. I think I have said enough to explain my behavior in your office that winter afternoon thirty years ago, the last time I actually saw you.

It was at the end of your day; it was already dark. I came into the waiting room just as your last patient was leaving and I didn't have time to sit down and compose myself. The receptionist ushered me into your office and a few minutes later you came in, still wearing your white coat. You paused at the doorway, peering at me over the rims of your spectacles. I remember how tired you looked. I had never seen you look tired before.

I remember how strange it seemed to be sitting in your office without anything physically wrong with me. I was emotionally tense, but I was not physically frightened and this made everything seem different. The office itself seemed smaller, your desk less massive. Still, when you spoke, it was your old voice, coming out of the mythic depths.

"Your mother told me you've changed your mind about going into medicine," you said as you took your seat behind the desk.

My God, you were so human! You were like a professor, or one of the doctors at the hospital, just another person, external to me. It was only when you spoke that the old dream awoke in me—each time as if for the first time and as if it had never disappeared. It was not what you said; it was somehow the sound of your voice, its vibration and timbre.

At the same time, all your gestures and your phrases seemed so empty and mechanical. How could I have ever believed in them? The stethoscope around your neck seemed only a meaningless prop.

Do you remember how I answered you?

"I had the wrong idea about medicine," I said, and I was shocked to hear how hollow my own words sounded. But I continued, "I was naive. I expected everyone to be like you."

Did I observe you smiling in modest embarrassment? Of course I did. But I was so young. I was stunned to see you affected by my adulation. Neither of us knew—how could we—what it was that I loved in you.

You swiveled your chair and started shuffling through some papers on the desk. Suddenly, you lifted your eyes and looked at me. I felt myself growing small. "Don't you think it's a little too soon to pass judgment on the whole of medicine?"

I felt small, but the sound of your voice made me feel large. What was it about your voice? I understand that now, but of course I did not understand it then. Do you know that in that moment I was ready to reverse my decision and commit myself again to becoming a doctor?

The telephone rang. You answered it without a moment's hesitation and in that same voice spoke reassuringly to a patient at the other end of the line. I heard you using phrases that had always meant so much to me, that had always helped me so much. Down deep in my body the sound of your voice was touching me in the same organic place that had been penetrated by the death of Mr. Patterson. But at the same time, I was observing your automatic techniques, your customary phrases. This repelled me even as your voice attracted me, or rather, attracted something in me, a sense of *being*.

As I say, I understand this now. I understand that the role of the physician had brought you experiences and a degree of inner power that you yourself did not understand or appreciate. That inner power, that inner human development was reflected in the sound of your voice, and had been so even years before when you were only a young doctor just starting out on your own, facing life and death, disease, suffering, with so much less of the armamentarium of modern technology and less of the social organization and pressures of contemporary medicine.

In any case, that winter afternoon in your office, I seemed to have met you when you were in transit, moving between eras of our whole culture. I saw you—hard to explain how I saw it—I saw you *believing* in your apparatus, your telephone, your very furniture, doctor! I know this sounds absurd to you, but it is what I felt and saw in that afternoon with you. I had no way of seeing how you were toward the whole mass of medical technology that was just then everywhere beginning to take the place of intuition. This was 1953. I was eighteen. You were just turning forty. You were between eras. The whole world was between eras—or, rather, was just entering the last, culminating phase of the modern era that has now ended and has left everyone, all of us, bereft of convictions and that has made seekers of us all, even you, doctor, even of you in your old age. Am I not right?

I had said I expected everyone to be like you and you had gently rebuked me for generalizing my first reactions. But can you now say that I was wrong—seeing what has become of your calling? Didn't I make the right decision? But perhaps you don't like anything of what I'm saying. You are an old man now; but are you an old man? I have heard nothing from you. Are you alive? Are you reading these letters?

5. Attention

You *are* there! My heart leaped when I saw your name on the envelope this morning.

Your letter tells me very little. No matter. The main thing is contact with you—I'm in touch with you. I even dream of seeing you again!

Concerning myself, I can be brief. I became a professor of philosophy without ever looking back, although I have never gone far away from my love of science and medicine. Of course, this statement would strike you as odd if I were to tell you the titles of the books I've written and the courses I've taught over the past quarter of a century. But I assure you, my interest in metaphysical questions is of one piece with my love of scientific knowledge. If I say that the ancient teachings have made it possible for me to love science even more, would you think me mad?

But now that I've made contact with you, that is exactly what I want to tell you. Had I written you a courteous little note, your reply would not have meant so much to me. I'm not especially interested in striking up new friendships, nor even in rekindling old friendships. To be blunt, I already have more than enough superficial friendships in my life. So I want to go on being direct with you. You've answered, even seeing what is in these letters. May I assume that you've answered not only out of nostalgia for an old patient? It's been thirty years now and you surely meant more to me than I did to you. May I hope that you've answered because something interests you in what I'm saying? In any case, that is going to be my assumption, even at the risk of not cultivating a really sweet set of memories.

I am saying that the ancient teachings about man and the universal order, just those teachings that modern science was supposed to have supplanted, have actually enabled me to love science once again. This did not happen all at once. My earlier days as a student of philosophy and then as a student of Oriental metaphysics at first caused me to feel contempt for modern science. But I eventually was helped to see that it was only the arrogance of the scientists that I hated, especially when this arrogance was expressed in the form of so-called scientific theory. I saw that there are very few genuine scientific theories in our time, although there is an overwhelming, wondrous and even glorious body of scientific fact. And if the so-called theories are needed like carrots on a stick for the scientists to bring home these glorious facts, well then I say, quoting a great teacher, "let them, let them!"

If I were to express myself lyrically, I would say that our era has long needed a new revelation to replace the worn-out religions of our culture and that the discoveries of the scientists, all taken together, constitute one-half of this new revelation. I mean that the facts brought by science constitute one-half of this revelation. The theories of science, however, cancel out the impact of these facts. They prevent these empirical discoveries about nature from awakening the certainty of meaning in the cosmos and in human life. And only when man feels the certainty of meaning is there activated in him the beginning of what is properly called intelligence and understanding. And only from intelligence and understanding does right action arise. Thus, as my studies of ancient— or, to be precise, preancient—ideas reached a specific stage, I began to experience the process whereby my attention was guided with the help of great ideas to a direct relationship to scientific facts. I experienced moments when great ideas replaced so-called theories.

I will give you an example, from my experience, of how universal ideas have helped me to see facts more clearly than the theories of modern science. This example is drawn from the field of psychiatry, and I hesitate only because, remembering you to be a man of common sense, I suspect you may not think very much of this branch of medicine.

It was in 1961, just after I had submitted my doctoral dissertation to the Yale University Department of Philosophy. I had recently returned from a year in Munich and found that, through some misunderstanding or petty treachery, I was without the teaching appointment I had counted on, and it was too late in the academic year to look elsewhere. Being newly married and without money, I was fairly desperate. As a last-ditch measure, I decided to apply to the psychiatry service of the local VA hospital where I had given one or two informal talks about the subject of my thesis, existential psychiatry. After one of my talks, the psychiatrist who was chief of the service, Dr. Louis B. Fierman, had half-jokingly offered me a job as—so he put it—"resident metaphysician."

I decided to call him on it and to my amazement he agreed, without a moment's hesitation, to take me on. I was to be classified as a "third-year clinical psychology trainee" with a salary considerably better than what I would have made as a philosophy instructor! That, by the way, was my initiation into the wonders of government spending.

I had absolutely no idea what my duties would be. I imagined I would simply hang out on the psychiatric wards pretending to do "research" under some grandiloquent designation such as "phenomenological-existential analyses of the world view of the schizophrenic." Why not? That I was hired at all was strange enough. This was a place where real help was needed for people with real suffering. If they were going to pay me real money for what I knew about an impenetrable German philosopher (Heidegger) and his almost equally impenetrable follower (the Swiss psychiatrist Binswanger), then anything was possible. Of one thing I was certain: All the metaphysical ideas I had studied and about which I had written so learnedly were of absolutely no practical use.

Are you smiling at all this, doctor? Believe me, so was I—in between moments of thanking God for handing me this sinecure. Who said roast chickens do not fly into your mouth? However, my happiness was not to last.

On the first day, I was given a private office, a white coat and a little name tag saying "Dr. Jacob Needleman"—I who had not yet even been officially awarded my Ph.D. in *philosophy*! Strolling around the corridors wearing this coat and name tag, I was immediately on the receiving end of the extraordinary respect people used to feel (and still do, in their hearts!) for anyone who is a doctor. It was a heady sensation. Once, even, a patient stopped me to ask about some physical complaint and I have to confess that I reacted by soberly advising him to get some rest and see how he felt the following morning. He thanked me profusely.

My office was a large, square room painted in a pessimistic shade of green and furnished only with a metal desk, three metallic padded chairs, and a lumpy sofa. It was located within the locked ward where the chronic and violent patients were housed. One of the young psychiatric residents advised me to assume the "parson's posture" when I walked through the ward— hands grasping the lapels of my white coat. This posture, he said, enables one most quickly to put up one's guard in case of physical attack. "It also makes you look like you know something," he added. I thanked him.

For the first three days I spent half my time in my new office spinning out exotic plans for interviewing patients in order to ascertain every detail of their way of perceiving reality. As an existential phenomenologist, my method was to resist making judgments about the truth or falsity of the patients' perceptions in order to intuit the main and central theme of their lives, their "world project," as it was called in this school of thought. The existential phenomenologists believed, and still believe, that scientific psychiatry, as epitomized by Freud, fails to understand the mentally ill patient from within. Using the categories of thought elaborated by the philosopher Martin Heidegger, they seek instead to grasp the fullness of what they take to be each individual's freely chosen structure of experience. They consider it a mistake to assume that the scientific world view is the basis of judging the validity of another human being's perceptions, no matter how wild and bizarre they may appear to be. In those days, I was a fervent believer in this school of thought and so I was all the more surprised, as I actually began observing and interacting with these patients, to hear myself saying under my breath such things as "this guy is really nuts." I kept such thoughts to myself.

Most of the rest of my time was spent idling in the hospital cafeteria, talking to the psychiatric staff who listened with great interest to my plans and theories. I was surprised and pleased at their openness and respect for what I had to say about psychiatry. But it also made me uneasy, which I attributed to the fact that I really did not know what I was talking about. Only later did I realize that my uneasiness had another cause, closely related to the first—namely, I was unconsciously perceiving that these medical specialists had no real conviction about the truth or effectiveness of their own knowledge. At the time, however, the result of my conversations with the psychiatric staff was that I began to believe I really understood something about the human psyche and its aberrations.

During these first days I also managed to conduct several long interviews with some of the patients diagnosed as "chronic schizophrenics." These psychotic men generously offered me a treasure chest of chaotic thought associations, quirky facial expressions, and random emotional outbursts, all of which I noted down with compassionate respect for their as yet undesignated "freely chosen world project."

One morning toward the end of my first week, the chief of the psychiatric service came into my office. Dr. Lou Fierman was a short, stocky man in his mid-forties with grizzled hair and pleasant, cleanly chiseled features. He had that certain look about him that administrators sometimes have after years of living through every possible kind of compromise, a look that in their best moments approaches the appearance of the kind of wisdom you sometimes sense in a simple, down-to-earth farmer or peasant who has seen through the naive illusions of his more cultured fellow men who do not really know how things actually happen in the world.

He sat down on the sofa and after a few minutes of pleasant chitchat, he came to the point of his visit.

"We've been talking about you," he said, "and we think you should take on a few patients of your own."

"What do you mean?" I answered, terror already engulfing me. I knew very well what he meant.

"We think you should do therapy."

Me? I? Do therapy? With real people? I stood for a moment in front of the concrete fact that I knew nothing about mental illness, about the mind, about people, about the real human condition. At the same time, my celebrated existentialist-phenomenological theory, which had only recently formed itself into a brilliant doctoral dissertation of publishable quality, gave off a depressingly feeble little light far, far off in the distance of my mind, utterly unrelated to the thunderous fact that I understood nothing about the human mind.

"But I've never had the slightest practical experience doing psychotherapy. Aren't you afraid I might hurt these patients?" My protest ended less vigorously than it had begun as two internal influences started acting on me, each from differemt regions of my own mind. On the one side, the sense of adventure and challenge started to lift my spirits with the prospect of exploring the unknown and learning something new about man. From the other side of my mind, the feeble light of the existentialist-phenomenological theory suddenly began to glow more brightly as a sort of voice whispered to me: "You, Jerry Needleman, you really do understand a considerable amount—are you not almost an offical Ph.D., trained at Harvard and Yale?" As I now realize, these two influences, so utterly different in their origin and nature—the former rooted in the honorable desire for truth and the latter rooted in vanity—mixed with each other in such a way that the love of truth became fueled by the energy of the ego. In that moment I became a living metaphor of the fate of knowledge itself in the modern world!

The last shreds of humility—that is to say, the last remaining trace of an accurate measure of my own powers—were swept away by the next remark of Dr. Fierman, a remark whose wisdom I instantly recognized even as my exaggerated estimate of myself began bubbling through me like carbonated water.

"Harm them?" he said, his face breaking out in a broad smile. "You can't possibly harm them! If we could harm them, then we could help them!"

That is what I remember him saying, though he undoubtedly did not intend it to sound so stark. I was practically thrown back in my chair by this remark. I could feel my eyes widening. Of course. Nobody here knows anything and nobody can do anything. The feeling of objective truth touched me deeply and I became intensely quiet inside. I tell you, doctor, it was a feeling not at all unlike the experience of seeing Mr. Patterson die, which I described to you in my previous letter.

I had studied much Eastern and Western philosophy, but only at that moment did I first begin to understand the idea spoken of by all the great sages of antiquity that men live their lives enmeshed in a web of illusions. But, and here is the point, the awakening of my understanding of this objective truth died aborning. I smiled back at Dr. Fierman and then shared a hearty laugh with him at the absurdity of all things. And, as I now realize, even in that good-natured laughter I lost touch with that real fragment of objective truth—namely, the clear and distinct certainty that we human beings are lived passively by forces that we do not see and that the perceptions and categories by which we experience ourselves correspond not at all to those forces. The things we think we do and the things that seem to happen to us are simply not real. I believe that Dr. Fierman, like the good householder of the ancient teachings, had come to understand this truth in his bones. And I ask you, doctor, don't all really good physicians understand this sooner or later?

As our laughter subsided, Dr. Fierman said to me, "You've read and studied more books about psychotherapy than anyone else on the service. Why not get some practical experience? Don't worry, we'll be here to supervise you, just like any other trainee."

His words completely soothed me, and by the time he left my

office, I was ready to slay giants. I very nearly said, "Bring me your toughest case!"

Let me remind you why I am telling you all this. I want to show you how my experience as a psychotherapist made me realize, of course only on the basis of reflections that took place much later in my life, how much knowledge is brought to us by modern medical science and how we actually pass it by. Even the dubious science of psychiatry puts great and unprecedented truths right on our plate, but we don't swallow them. We don't even see them!

My first patient was a man named Molesky. He was a tall, incredibly timid man of about fifty-five with a receding hairline and tiny, watery eyes. He squinted as he entered my office and shuffled to the chair next to my desk. His problem, he said in a near whisper, was his trembling hands. And, in fact, his hands resting in his lap, were constantly jerking around like two small, frightened mice.

I began to ask him every sort of question about his thoughts and feelings, his past, his childhood, his experiences in the army. At a certain point, he simply fell silent and refused to speak for the rest of the hour. The following day, he told me about his father's suicide attempt a few years earlier and about his difficulties with his wife. And once again, halfway through the session, he stopped talking and we sat together for a very long time in silence until I indicated the end of the hour. This pattern persisted for four months, until Mr. Molesky finally got up and left in mid-session with the words, "This isn't doing me any good."

My second patient, brought to me a few days after I started with Mr. Molesky, was a bright black man named Tom Leonard, forty-one years old. Unlike Molesky, Mr. Leonard poured forth a cornucopia of information about himself and his problems. "I live in a fallacy world," he said. "I am unsure of the validity of my ideas." Mr. Leonard's problem was that he heard voices and was constantly picking up radio messages in his brain. These messages dealt with important personages such as the president and also contained songs that he said he had composed but that had actually been plagiarized from a certain popular singer named Vic Damone.

I heard a great deal about Mr. Leonard's childhood, especially two incidents—one in which he sicked his family dog on a mailman, the result of which was that the dog severely bit the boy and was then shot by the patient's father, and the other in which he was taught about masturbation from a neighborhood girl five or six years older than he.

There were several other patients as well, but the long and the short of it was that within two weeks I became intensely bored with the whole enterprise. I looked with dismay upon the months stretching ahead in which I would be forced to listen to these patients every day.

When I had to make a case presentation before the staff of the psychiatric service, I gathered together my notes about Mr. Leonard and created a "world design" that was in a way a piece of pure fiction, but which I offered as the central theme characterizing the patient's perceptions of his world. To my amazement, the presentation was greeted with enthusiasm and applause by the staff of trained, experienced psychiatrists and psychologists. And at one point during this farce, I saw Dr. Fierman looking on with an expression of quiet, ironic amusement, as though he were watching children at play. That reminded me for a moment of my conversation with him and the liberating realization it had brought me that no one of us knew or could possibly know anything real about the human psyche.

Although my boredom continued unabated, I began devoting great energy to reading and rereading everything I could get my hands on about psychiatry, especially the theories of Freud. In addition, I began observing the work of my colleagues through a one-way mirror. I was both shocked and depressed to see how these experienced psychotherapists conducted the sessions with their patients. They floundered about exactly as I did, even though they showed a certain professional calm in the process. But this only increased my desire to read more and to observe more of their work. I was gripped by some kind of passion, which I can now formulate as follows: There must be some knowledge behind the practice of psychotherapy. Somewhere, somehow, at some point in its development, there must have existed and may still exist, some piece of real understanding about human suffering and its alleviation. But what was that knowledge? Hundreds, thousands of psychotherapists exist throughout the world along with even greater numbers of patients. Surely some need was being met. But what? And how?

Observing the practice of the psychiatrists through the one-way mirror, I was soon struck by one great contradiction. Subconsciously, I received the indelible impression that all of them were doing the same thing in exactly the same way, the only difference consisting in the tiniest variations of words, postures, and timbre of the voice. Yet when I discussed their work with them and when I met with my training supervisors, I was informed about the great differences in approach and method, based on differences in the theories they adopted about the dynamics of the mind and the causes of mental illness. There were the "strict Freudians," "the neo-Freudians," the followers of the "client-centered" approach, and so on. Subconsciously, all that I could detect was that some had their patients lying on a couch and others had them sitting in a chair; some said little, others said more; some spoke seriously to their patients, others joked and bantered; some probed the past of the patient, others tried to reflect the patient's present reactions and thoughts. These variations struck me as absolutely trivial—that is to say, I sensed the triviality of these differences deep down in my "guts." At the same time, however, as a good student and moreover as a student desperately trying to be interested in my job, I became persuaded mentally that these differences were important. And I tried to vary my own approach to my patients accordingly.

As I see now, however, it was my gut feeling that propelled my investigations. I already knew, down deep, that my celebrated "existential-phenomenological" approach was only another tiny variation of whatever it was that all these methods had in common. Yet on the surface, I was obliged to present this approach and myself as representing an alternative method deserving to rank along with the "strict Freudianism," "neo-Freudianism," "client-centered" approach, and so on. To be exact, I became a professional anti-Freudian.

But down deep, as I say, sub- or semiconsciously, I sensed that Freud was the only real source of energy in the entire cultural movement called psychiatry and psychotherapy. At the same time, my study of the theories of Freud—which I had undertaken in great detail for my doctoral thesis and which I again repeated in the present circumstances—showed me nothing that could really explain his vast influence. Time and again, reading his writings, I would catch myself beginning to grow excited by his ideas about the play of forces within the mind. But when I put down the book, it was as though I was suddenly waking from a dream. His theories had life for me only when I was reading his writings. But when I was not reading his writings, they seemed—at best— ingeniously constructed speculations with a distinctively depressing effect on my whole being.

I soon realized what was behind all this—again, not fully consciously to myself. I said to myself in so many words: It is his *style* that excites me, that gives me hope. His style is what has made him such a vast influence. His style is his energy.

It is very strange, you will admit. But I am willing to spend as long as you wish to prove the truth of what I'm saying. But first, hear me out. Freud's style, his energy, his passion is of another level than his thoughts. It is the style of the true physician!

Looking back on this now, I see that I had actually solved the mystery of Freud, but I didn't realize how complete and important this solution was. I didn't have the words for it, I mean, the ideas, the comprehension that this was the answer to the riddle of Freud that, for me, had become like the riddle of the Sphinx— as Freud called it himself when he attempted to explain the meaning of dreams in his first great book.

But books alone do not bring positive change in human lives, far less in human history. And that psychiatry had in it a positive, beneficent force had by now become a certainty for me, however begrudgingly and vaguely I admitted it to myself. And so I more or less asked myself: What was it in Freud himself that was so good, so beneficent for his patients and that was sensed by and perhaps to some extent even transmitted to those who knew him as their teacher? Freud was an authentic physician. He was actually able to help those poor men and women the likes of whom, as I remember my good Dr. Fierman observing, *we* can neither help nor harm. Why was he such an effective doctor? What had he really discovered? This was the bedrock question about Freud, the real riddle. How could a man whose theoretical constructs about the human psyche were so complicated and artificial be such a good physician?

You may wish to dispute my claim about the powerlessness of books. But remember, I am speaking of the power to produce positive change in people's lives, and so I don't deny that books can bring new fantasies or even new ideas that concentrate the falling energy of a particular era and channel it into an explosion. Our era's absurd predilection for psychology—or, if you prefer, our era's predilection for absurd psychology—is an example of such an explosion, harmless when compared to the influence of a *Das Kapital*, say, but nonetheless a serious factor among all those other causes in our culture that prevent people from living in the real world.

I wish to state flatly that all books that have had a positive influence in human life have been such only because of the personal being of their authors or because of interpreters who themselves have been influenced directly and personally either by the author or by some exceptional life circumstance. Among such books, I include, of course, our Bible as well as great works of philosophy, science, and literature. Such books are the image of their creator who himself, or through his circle of direct and indirect pupils, radiates something real and tangible into the life of people. When that inner, real vibration disappears—that is, when these books are used solely by men and women who have not received the personal force of the author—then even these books, perhaps especially these books, become a destructive influence in the lives of men and women. Witness the uses of our Bible, to name only the most obvious example.

What was it about Freud himself? What did he really discover? What was in the man that was reflected in his writings? I knew there was something very powerful and real eluding me, and eluding everyone else I met, including the "orthodox Freudians."

Bear with me, my story is almost over. In fact, *I did not discover what I was looking for.* At the same time, I see now that I had actually solved the riddle of Freud; it was right in front of me, but I had not the ideas or experience with which to take it in and make it part of my conscious understanding. Freud had made a truly great scientific discovery, but I couldn't see it clearly. Consequently, my professional anti-Freudianism became even more intense.

When people claimed that Freud's great discovery was the unconscious, I bridled. It was true, but it was not true. Freud's theories of the unconscious were riddled with prejudices and naive metaphysical assumptions based on the then current mythologies of biology. When they said he had explained the psyche in terms of ancient myths and symbols, I also bridled in front of the fact that these interpretations reduced the universe of nature to a stupid play of blind forces all less mindful and purposeful than the Freudian ego itself. When people singled out his discovery of the transference phenomenon in psychotherapy, I yawned, even while sensing the electricity of this idea. It, too, was true and not true. The patient did live out the patterns of his psyche in relationship to the therapist, but that still left out the question of what was the healing force in the process. When the answer was given—the patient becomes aware of his motivations and complexes—I yawned even more because the whole question was how that so-called awareness really healed anything at all—having witnessed myself more than enough so-called awareness in the patients of my colleagues and supervisors. "Awareness" was a very plentiful commodity on the sixth floor of the VA hospital. But not a single bit of this "awareness," which flowed like water from an open tap, had the slightest healing effect on the patients. Yet most of the psychiatrists and psychotherapists were not only dedicated professionals, highly trained and highly educated, but many were even strict Freudians—and indeed one was a Freudian of the old school, having been trained in Vienna.

Finally, those who referred to Freud's unique "charisma" were, to my mind, simply confessing intellectual bankruptcy. Of course, Freud had "charisma," but the whole point was to know the nature of that special quality in the man that actually helped to free people from the prison of their exaggeratedly interlocking negative emotions, a condition aptly named "neurosis."

After my year at the VA hospital was over, I left and returned to academic philosophy. It was not until ten years had passed that I began to see what it was about Freud that had been so close to me that it was invisible. And it was not until another ten years had passed that the remainder of the mystery, and the most important part of it, was finally solved.

I am taking so much time to tell you all this not only because of what I want to say about Freud and his discovery but principally because of what this story illustrates about the discoveries of modern science—namely, that science, especially medical science, has indeed made it possible to know and understand the human body in health and illness, but its discoveries are largely unappreciated, even by doctors and scientists themselves! I mean to say: unappreciated, because unseen. We have enough knowledge, maybe even more than enough knowledge, but who understands and appreciates it? No one really knows what is important and what is secondary in all the discoveries of modern science. There is no conviction, no morality in our cognitive processes. We don't feel what we know!

So let me go on with this story, which has now become not only longer than I originally intended but longer than I intended two pages ago. About ten years after I returned to the academic profession, the wife of a colleague and close friend of mine experienced a mental breakdown and attempted suicide. Knowing my background, my friend implored me to suggest a good psychiatrist for her and after a great deal of pondering, I realized, to my surprise, that had I myself been in such need—either for myself or for my loved ones—I would have had no hesitation in putting myself in the hands of Freud were he alive. All I could do for my friend was to suggest a therapist I knew who happened to be a kindly and sympathetic human being, but realizing my esteem for Freud caused me to reawaken my interest in the riddle of Freud, especially as I was writing and lecturing on themes having to do with the ancient teachings about the human mind.

To put it briefly, I came to the conclusion that the greatness of Freud was due mainly to the fact that he was looking at the mind and at the suffering of his patients with an intensity that arises only when all one's own deeply rooted opinions are destroyed. Freud, in a word, had a tiger by the tail. He had the good fortune, like many of the founders of modern science, to be what is conventionally called a "genius"—that is, to have a good education and a very active intellectual brain—and with this "genius" of his to have stumbled into an area of inquiry in such a way as to be forced to let go of every assumption and opinion that was ever held about it. This combination of being a decently moral man and being committed to solve a problem for which there were absolutely no ready-made answers to be found anywhere produced in him a power of mind that enabled him to see and act with revolutionary effectiveness, objectivity, and compassion.

That was my discovery. I realized, at the same time, that not even the great Freud was aware of how important this factor was in his own scientific development—I mean, the factor of having a tiger by the tail, which I would define as the state of consciousness that appears when, with all one's being, one realizes that one does not understand and, at the same time, with all one's heart recognizes that one must absolutely and imperatively reach understanding. I can tell you now that this condition of the psyche was given very precise names by the masters of the ancient teachings, such as Socrates and Pythagoras, as well as by those teachers whose names have, unfortunately in my view, become associated with the dregs of certain belief systems that we recognize as religious dogmas. In this connection, I will only cite such names as Meister Eckhart, the Ba'al Shem Tov, Jalalluddin Rumi, and the Tibetan saint, Milarepa.

How could Freud have recognized the centrality of this factor? Of course, he could not. He was utterly alone. And so, not recognizing this factor and its primary importance in his successful dealings with his patients, he was unable to transmit to others, except accidentally and in piecemeal fashion, what he found. In this, the great Freud—yes, even Freud, the paradigm of faith in scientific reasoning—resembles those unusual men and women throughout the ages who have experienced authentic moments of contact with a qualitatively higher energy of mind and have stumbled badly, even with the best intention, in communicating their discoveries. Freud, like Newton and Kepler and perhaps even Darwin and certainly Einstein, was half a mystic and half a scientist. Had he been 100 percent mystic, he could then have been also 100 percent scientist. But, as it was, he falls into the same category, in my opinion, as other notable and influential half-mystics throughout history who attain something great without knowing how or why they attained it and who then reach for the nearest concepts or images in order to express what they have attained—be it religious concepts, artistic images, or, as in Freud's case, biological theories. The current of semimysticism, which has had such regrettable effects in the history of the Christian religion, continued its course under the banner of science, culminating in the influence of Freud.

But many years had to pass before I understood exactly what Freud had discovered in this psychic condition I have described. I can now give it a name: *attention*. Having a tiger by the tail, Freud was able to look at himself and his patients with a power of attention that is only rarely experienced in the ordinary life of people. This force of attention appears when through a great shock or a situation of total urgency, all the routine functions of the whole human mind release the higher energies held captive by them. In fact, as you are reading this, doctor, there are researchers in the field of brain physiology who are knocking at the door of discovering that there are cells in the human brain specifically designed to work with this higher energy.

The unbound energy of attention that Freud emanated to his patients was the healing factor. But the theoretical constructs he invented in order to explain his own results are completely inadequate to this phenomenal capacity of the human organism to serve as a conduit for the creation of unbound attention that, in the mystical teachings of the Judaic tradition is called *Da'at*, the divinely mobile consciousness.

But even had he put this discovery of his into his theories, the result would have been no better unless he had understood exactly how and through what inner experiences he had reached this rare power of the mind within himself.

I will go no further, except to say that the followers of Freud inevitably turned to theory, which is precisely that in the mind that, among other factors, captures and binds this phenomenal energy; therefore there was nothing in Freudianism that gave the possibility of there arising another Freud. It was inevitable that, compared to Freud's successes, no real healing could be instituted within the techniques of modern psychiatry.

A study of the history of medicine is needed to show how the evocation of this power of unbound attention and *redirected* attention lies behind the otherwise incomprehensible and apparently primitive, superstitious methods of ancient physicians. This study would show, I believe, that this is the reason why ancient systems of medicine are usually contained within the embrace of the great psychospiritual religious teachings of the past, as it is there in these spiritual-religious systems that the recognition of this power of the mind is found—under many names, most of which are symbolic and mythic, in accordance with the fact that this great power of the mind arises not only, and not principally, out of the intellectual function but also out of the emotional and motor functions of the human organism.

But now I must stop. Or shall I go on?

6. The Last Guardian

I am writing again, without waiting for your reply to my last letter, to reiterate that my only wish is simply to make contact with you, to hear from you, to see you once again. Please do not feel you have to respond to anything specific in these letters. But only, please, respond.

Now that I have heard from you, I find myself imagining things about you. My last picture is of you about to be engulfed by the changes that have afflicted your entire profession. But right under that picture I still see you as I saw you when I was young.

In my mind, you are both of these pictures, you are *two*. You are a presence and a movement away from that presence into scientism, businessism, sportism, altruism, and all the other self-contained fragments that make up the sorrow of our culture.

I will not surrender my early image of you, no matter what. At the same time, I assure you that I recognize the power of the forces that have pulled you away. They are pulling me too.

We cannot resist these forces, this I understand. I, too, cheat and compromise at every turn. I cannot fill the roles I have to play in life—father, teacher, artist. I, too, am consumed by the merciless pressure of time, that most realistic of chimeras. My attention, too, is scattered and muddied like pure light diffused through a million pieces of broken glass.

New technologies constantly infiltrate my life like painted whores. They give me powers I never dreamt of and lure me away from the feeling of myself, by which feeling alone a man can live his life like a man. I confront the obligations of a man without the moral feelings of a man. And therefore I am bewildered by all the new knowledge being served up to us in this new world we are all entering.

Like you, I am powerfully drawn to this new knowledge. At last, we can do something, whereas before we could do nothing with that pathetic blend of piecemeal knowledge and disemboweled religion. But it is even more pathetic to have new knowledge while the feeble inner powers of our recent past themselves ebb farther and farther away from us. We cannot and we do not wish to give up this new world. But, doctor of my childhood, we need the Being within ourselves that can make this new knowledge a force for the common good.

I will not try now to summarize all that is pulling on us in this new world, drawing us into the surface automatisms of our psyche, cementing us in an egoism over against which the great forces of Nature can no longer patiently look on like an indulgent mother, but instead stands poised to act decisively and visibly like an angry father.

I want to say only this, that you alone, of all people in this new world, still stand at the gate of the reality of that one experience which can bring every man and woman in front of the question of Being—namely the experience of death and the mortal body.

No matter how far we are pulled into the illusion of this new world, still each of us must die. This towering fact of death is the only metaphysical truth left to us and you are its guardian. Yet from this one truth, the whole meaning and aim of human life can be reconstructed because in front of this fact, as the greatest of the ancients knew, the desire for both life and meaning arises in us. The desire to live forever, to not die, to not disappear into the dust, arises in human consciousness in front of the fact of death.

Do not drug us into dreams of immortality without meaning.

Do not encourage us to sleep in the ever-new illusions of the mortal body.

Support in us the wish for Being that is the real, authentic human expression of the wish to not die that is inscribed in everything that lives.

We all live in the same, difficult world. Help us, by the example of your own search, to attend to this difficult new world as an exercise in self-knowledge.

Before the fact of death, each of us divides naturally into two—a presence and a movement away from this presence. Before the fact of death, each of us sees all that was of such importance to us as existing only in one part of ourselves, that part that is soon destined to be dissolved forever.

As a philosopher, I have come to understand the goal of life as the effort to individualize something in myself that can nourish this presence through the very energies that are spent so lavishly in the activities of my everyday life. This something is individual Being.

But I am only a philosopher. I can tell you about your scientific knowledge and the great truths hidden in it—but it is you who must feel these truths in your actions with your suffering neighbor. I can tell you about the pressures and fears of everyday living in this new world, this cultural revolution we have entered. But it is you who must individualize Being in yourself.

As a philosopher who is also seeking to be an individual man, I have understood how useless it is to speak too soon of God, that term that means only the general, abstract, all-pervasive Being of all beings. This God, I now see, must meet this mortal body in an actual physical contact, an actual blending of the two distinct currents of reality that flow for the brief space of a lifetime within the confines of this miraculous mechanism called the human body—this human body that is intended as the stage for the individualization of God.

Well, doctor, my cards are all on the table.

7. On Courage and Authority

I was hurrying out the door when your long letter arrived. I put it in my pocket and snatched glances at it during the day in between appointments, lectures and conferences. Only now, late at night, have I been able to set everything aside and read it carefully.

You joke about how busy you are. You say it is unseemly for a man of your "advanced years" to be doing so much. And then, out of nowhere it seems, you use the word *courage*. You are president of this, director of that, administrator of this and that, consultant, chairman, editor. It takes "courage," you say, just to be a doctor and treat patients. Medicine has become a vast, complex business organization—with a huge department of research and development, another of financial administration, another of publishing, fund raising, public relations, and so on.

Don't worry, I hear what is in your letter. I promise you, you will not have to play at being a philosopher with me. I know what the administrative structure of modern life is and what it means. You are speaking about the technology of living itself. This administrative structure *is* our culture, our form of life in the contemporary world.

If you have a heart or a soul—or whatever they used to call man's essence in olden times—you are going to express it through the channels of the corporate structure of your life, your work, your calling. Just as businesses have no Department of Metaphysical Search, medicine has no residencies or examining boards of "inwardness." You will find a way to seek, to penetrate into reality, within your corporate structure, however. You must find a way. So must I.

It is our culture we are speaking of, our basic environment of living. Modern life is organized along the lines of a business. I, a so-called philosopher (what a quaint word!), spend as much time at the Xerox machines as you do. I also, all of us do, fill out forms, run to and fro between my desk and my filing cabinet where my affairs are arranged alphabetically and, within individual items, according to date received. Or, lately, and more and more, to and fro between my life and the computer.

The whole thing—not only capitalism but also Marxism, and also of course the gathering of knowledge, the producing of art, the education of children—the whole thing—eating, drinking, sleeping, making love—all of it is rationlized, organized according to binary logic, the logic of the computer. The computer is the Pentateuch of modern man. The computer is what our dear Hegel would have called the Notion made concrete—that is to say, it is our era finally become conscious of itself in history and matter.

Really, it is nothing to complain about, but it is something we need to see and understand. Otherwise, we will never be free of it, never be able confidently to touch the organic logic, the physical logic of reality, the logic of God and his creation.

Business and science are one and the same thing. They have so converged in our culture. We are all under the sway of the computer and have been so for quite some time, long before the computer was invented.

Our lives have become businesses. John Smith, Inc., Mary Jones, Inc. The question of how to live has become the hunt for psychosomatic software. The Ten Commandments? No, the divine algorithm—the divine decision procedure. Everywhere and in everything, decision procedures—rules—are taking the place of Laws. And nothing is better at articulating rules than the computer mind. Allow me to say it again: Instead of Moses with the Ten Commandments inscribed in stone, stone being a perduring permanence formed by Nature (God) itself, we are under the sway of algorithms maintained by the fragile and miniscule electric current necessary to preserve the memory banks of the computer mind.

So I very well understand that you have so little time, doctor. In everything you give your time to, you find—we find—there is too little time. We are all on the way to the disappearance of time entirely, which means the disappearance of being entirely. The present moment is getting smaller and smaller—at first hours, as in the "admirably" organized overlarge monasteries and universities of the Middle Ages, to the quarter hours struck by the Venetian clocks for the first time in history at the precise convergence of capitalism and Protestant rationalism, to the second hand on our clocks, and even to the tenth and hundredth of a second on our digital watches.

Time is energy—such is the message of very ancient teachings that recognized ordinary conceptions of time as illusory and subjective. Illusory—I am just beginning to understand what that word means. It means a belief that masks my lack of presence and is therefore an integral part of my egoism. An illusion is a belief that says "I." Such beliefs may or may not be dispelled by other beliefs—but the point is that the very structure of belief as such must be destroyed.

To create time is impossible without acquiring new energy. And the illusion of rationalism is that decision procedures save something—save time, save energy. Quite the contrary is true because believing in decision procedures, the wrong trust in the computer mind, actually diminishes the energy in our lives and activities. Therefore the quality of time is degraded. The tempo of our lives and activities becomes more and more inhuman.

It is the same thing for you as it is for me. Our lives are fragmented by separate pieces of knowledge, separate aims having no relationship to each other except for being under the sway of the inhuman tempo of inhuman energy. We don't know what is essential and therefore each passing aim appears essential to us when it is activated. We lurch from one thing to another, pausing only when some ineluctable organic reality such as death smashes into us or into someone close to us. We never give all our energy to any one thing, but instead we find that little spurts of energy go to hundreds and thousands of little aims. Many aims do not add up to one single great aim. There must be a center for there to be human life. There must be the essential in ourselves presiding over our work and life for there to appear a new and better quality of time. With a central human aim, the other pieces of our activity will naturally dispose themselves in its service. Then, time will again appear in our lives because we will know what we want, and we will know what we want only when that energy appears in us that can really will, that can really decide according to cosmic, natural Law.

I am not surprised that you wrote about the scientific advances of modern medicine in a tone that is part respectful and part rueful. You speak of the development of technology and the progressive diminution of clinical judgment with a feeling of weary resignation, as though the former is necessarily purchased at the expense of the latter. What have you lived through that gives you this perspective? I know the answer to that question, having seen you when you were just entering the tunnel of scientism and "seeing" you now as you blink your eyes at the other end, emerging from that tunnel only to discover that the countryside is not what you thought it would be.

Of course, you can't and don't want to go back through that tunnel. If my own experience is any basis, you don't have to, even if it were possible. But in order to bring the human quality back to our life and to our work—and by human quality I mean to include also knowledge and judgment, as well as finer feelings—we will have to struggle with ourselves in an entirely new way.

Please don't think me presumptuous to speak to you like this. Only judge what I say by its quality and make allowances for my relative youth. I have my own style, my own prison, after all. But I have discovered some things—with help.

For example, concerning time: I have found that real ethical choices create time by liberating energy that is usually trapped and exhausted by the automatic impulses of ego and "herd instinct." Real choices compel us to come back to ourselves, to come inside ourselves. This can take place in the kind of lives we lead only when we are in front of contradictory obligations along-side the demand for prompt action. In order for me to act freely, a free energy has to appear in me, an energy without form. In such moments, under such a demand, one sometimes clearly sees the hypnotic power of familiar so-called moral obligations. Such "moral obligations" may then be understood as the habitual forms human energy takes, sanctioned by society, but neverthe-less not free at all, not human in the deepest sense of the term.

This sort of inner freedom is the hidden meaning of such words as *altruism, love of knowledge, service to God and neighbor.* There exists in our language and our culture what might be called legends, myths, ancient stories about certain motivations that can act as the springs of human action. Such words are very like mythic gods who are supposed to exist among mortals and act in their lives, very like the ancient Greek gods. These gods exist in another realm, on another scale of time—they are "immortal" and ever-present forces. And the idea of the hero, the mythic superior man, who is he? Half mortal, half god, he conducts his life amid the same problems and compulsions as we mere mortals, but he also has contact with another kind of time and another kind of reality. His life and actions have authentic meaning be-cause he lives in two worlds at once, whereas we poor mortals live only in the world of "forms" and appearances.

The hero has to pay an immense price for his being, for his existence in two worlds, a price mere mortals are unprepared to pay. For example, he has to "die early" in order to enter the realm of "the eternal." He has to step outside the river of ordinary time, cast aside his "obligations," move outside "good and evil," as is also counseled in mythic terms by the book of Genesis.

Patience, doctor, patience. Let me go on. I know what I am speaking about and I assure you it is relevant—yes, even to your clinical judgment and to your busy life.

In speaking of the courage needed simply to practice direct medicine, I take you to mean a commitment to the relationship between a human doctor and his human patient. Throughout history, we can see that this relationship has been in varying ways one of the principal forms in which people have received some nourishment for their higher feelings. We see that medicine has been a part of culture in its authentic sense derived from the root word itself, *culture*—to nourish. So much else has been taken away from modern man in this respect—religion, family, ritual, the special quality of sacrifice embedded in the ancient external forms of human relationships and labor. You perhaps sense that the medical relationship must not go the way of all these forms. At least, that is how I see it. The medical relationship can be and, to some extent, still is a realm where some components of authentic human happiness can be cultivated.

I am very taken by your word, *courage*. Remember how you used to stand before a patient and, by the authority of your role and your presence, you would demand of him that he simply stop his life, if only for a certain time and to a certain extent. You yourself used to insert your patient into a new kind of time. Under your authority, we would give up this or that, diligently practice some regimen, surrender one or another tense "obligation," exercise some manner of serious self-discipline—and through such things experience the relativity of human life itself as we are lived by it in ordinary time. The technological achievements of modern medicine have almost entirely done away with this aspect of the medical relationship. In general, this has been the effect of advanced technology throughout our society—to strip away the last remaining factors of living that help an individual to sense and experience the relativity and transiency of human life. The impact of advanced technology has been to erase the metaphysical truths embedded in the forms of living handed down by our remote ancestors. And without metaphysics, man cannot live— that is to say, without some true impressions of his metaphysical nature, man cannot be moral or happy. We are transient beings, yet the desires and impulses of our transitory personalities can never be the factor that guides us to fulfillment. Our personalities are temporary structures erected like scaffolding around some as yet unfinished temple of imperishable being, a temple called, in the ancient teachings, the soul. In illness, man can let go of the scaffolding—a little, but this little is a great deal. He can at least see the scaffolding for what it is.

How to maintain this central and sacred meaning of suffering without giving up what is good and true in the great discoveries of modern science and technology? That, doctor, is surely the most important question of our era, and in this your profession has a fundamental role to play.

You once had the authority to lead another human being toward such experiences. Your authority was metaphysical and therefore moral. Our culture no longer believes in the reality of death and therefore no longer believes in the reality of immortality. But you once did believe in these things, you once understood.

And I know you agree with what I'm saying. I know that you have seen through the illusions of technology and the algorhythmic organization of our lives and work. You know men die amid CAT scanners, dialysis machines, and artificial hearts just as they have always died. You see through the illusions created by the organization of modern medicine in our complicated world. You will regain your authority and you will feel the reality of your responsibility when you remember what you know and what you have seen of life and death. Isn't this what you mean by "courage"? It will be in your eyes when people speak to you about such things as "equity in the delivery of health-care," medical corporations, or "patients' rights." Your eyes, which have seen life and death, will be steady and gentle because they are seeing another, wider horizon. You will not react to one thing and then to another thing and then to another thing. People will sense something in you. They will stop suing you, stop putting you on committees. They will feel your authority and, without knowing why, they will slowly rally to help you. And this will give you time. The whole world wants this of you, without knowing it. Because the whole world wants Being to be born in its midst, within people. And people will open to another human being who has this presence in him.

II. YOU PHYSICIANS

8. At the Threshold

I want to tell you what I have been trying with your colleagues here in California and then I want to ask your help about taking the next step with them. Frankly, I've come to the end of my rope. I've proved to myself that doctors want and need to face the existential questions associated with the practice of medicine. And I've proved to myself that I'm able to speak to them about such questions that, as I hope I've made clear, go beyond even the difficult problems of medical ethics that all of you now face— questions that deal not only with the meaning of medicine, but with the meaning of life itself.

But having proved all that to myself, I now find myself at a sort of threshold or interval that I think only an exchange with you can help me to cross. In fact, it is this state of affairs that has prompted me to write to you in the first place. The honest truth is that I'm in a bind and need your help.

It's true that I've gotten into these situations before. Sticking my neck out has become a habit with me. It all comes from a conviction that has somehow insinuated itself into my conscious-ness that more than anything else the influential people in our culture need to hear new ideas about man's place in the universal order and that these ideas can make a practical difference in how we conduct our lives. Years ago I made a vow that I would not stay within the protected confines of an academic environment. And so I've mixed with religious leaders, businessmen, philan-thropic organizations, scientists, psychiatrists, artists . . .

Speaking with people in all these different fields, there has always come a point where some special impulse was needed both from them and from myself in order for our exchanges to go beyond words or the mere evocation of good intentions and enthusiastic programs for action. I know from my own experience that the transformation of human consciousness, which is the only hope for individuals in our world, is never approached merely through evoking such reactions. Yet until now that is all I have succeeded in doing. In this sense, even though I have acquired a reputation for being able to speak about ideas, all my attempts to introduce such ideas in the actual lives of these people have been a failure.

I summarize the situation in the following way: To be a good doctor, one has first of all to be a good man. And to be a good man, one has to begin by discovering somewhere in oneself the desire for truth and to work at putting that desire above everything else in life, even, at the beginning, above the desire to help one's neighbor.

Summarizing further, I can say that my studies of this inner struggle to place the desire for truth above everything else inevitably brings an individual to the point where it is possible and necessary, in order to go further, for him to give careful attention to the welfare of his neighbor—that is to say, he must search for and attend with great care and diligence to those deep and organic impulses within himself to which the words *compassion* and *love* are justly applied.

In short, I have verified that in all realms of life with which I have had experience, truth is the only effective force. I have also verified that there is in human nature a deep inner attraction to truth, for its own sake. But I have not yet succeeded in calling this forth in people so that it actually becomes, if only a little, an active force in their lives and work.

It has been two years since I started working with various groups of physicians here in San Francisco. About three months ago—just before I wrote my first letter to you—I saw, with a jolt, that I had reached that interval or threshold at which all human enterprises either go forward with a new quality of energy or deviate from their original intention. It happened in the following way.

Starting in October of last year, I began to give a series of weekly seminars at the Gresham Memorial Medical Center under the title "Human Values in the Practice of Medicine." I realized that interest in this theme was connected with the practical dilemmas doctors were now coming up against due to the new medical technologies and the rising tide of negative public opinion about costs and about doctor-patient relationships.

I did not delude myself with the belief that physicians as a group were coming to great philosophical questions about the meaning of their own individual lives. But was it possible, I wondered, to speak about these practical ethical issues while at the same time introducing new universal ideas that would call those who heard them to the search for Truth?

That was how I expressed my project to myself. What arrogance! A quite wrong estimation of myself lay behind this way of setting my task. From the very outset, the realities of the situation began calling attention to themselves, but it took me a year to see them clearly. In the first place, it seemed I was dead wrong in assuming that my audience of doctors were not intensely interested in abstract philosophical ideas. On the contrary, whenever I started speaking about the nature of consciousness or metaphysics, a hushed attentiveness fell over them. But when I began speaking about questions that lay within their own field of experience—such as the problem of excessive reliance on technology or the problem of increasingly narrow fields of medical specialization—the meetings would turn into an outpouring of opinions, complaints, and arguments, with me playing the role, at best, of a kind of group psychotherapist. And I soon saw how helpless I was to bring them to the kind of ideas that have meant so much to me in my own life.

The shock in all this is the realization that it was *I*, not they, who kept steering the discussion away from ideas! I said to myself that my aim was to explore how the search for consciousness can be and needs to be conducted in the midst of practical life, yet the real fact was that at a certain point I always became afraid they would find metaphysics irrelevant.

Do you begin to see my difficulty, doctor? When I speak of an interval that needs to be crossed, I am speaking of myself and not only of you and your colleagues.

May I say that the whole modern world stands in front of this interval now, but perhaps it is especially clear in the science of medicine. For many decades, for centuries, the illusion of material and scientific progress has prevented mankind from facing this interval squarely. Just at the point where one comes against the limitations of one's being and state of consciousness, the thought captures us: more information, more technology, new theories— rather than the awareness that as we are, deep down, intrinsically, structurally, we can go no further toward the real betterment of human life. Mankind has turned away from this truth for centuries—and the extent of this turning away defines what it means to be a contemporary individual, without spiritual tradition in its real sense (not in the sense of outer forms or beliefs).

Yet, medicine, which brings man constantly in front of the fact of death, has remained, through it all, the last repository of the truth of the human condition. It was the first real science in the history of man because of this, and now, it seems, it may become the last science as it loses hold of this awareness. The illusion of material and scientific progress is creeping into places where one would never have dreamt it could go. An individual, in his individual life, spins round and round the same axis, repeating the same patterns, making the same mistakes. We spin, hundreds, thousands of times. But our time is not unlimited. Our life is part of a larger necessity; that is to say, we are finite. The whole of life on earth, of which we are part, itself moves in a certain direction and its purposes take us with it, even as we spin round and round. Eventually, we come to our last revolution, death. If we have not broken our pattern by then, it is too late for us. And the chief thing that prevents us from breaking this pattern are our dreams and illusions, our misrepresentations to ourselves of the nature and quality of our knowledge. But to break this pattern, to cease spinning round the same axis, requires that we cross, existentially cross, some extraordinary threshold, interval.

The planet earth also spins round its axis and revolves around its sun. And the sun also is moving, somewhere, we don't know where.

In between this immense movement of the earth around the sun and the tiny movements of individual man, there surely lies the purpose and meaning of the human race as a whole with all its activity on the surface of our planet. But what of our civilization with all its mental, emotional, and physical energy? Surely, mankind also spins and spins. And it is hard to avoid the supposition that, in a certain sense at least, civilization as we know it and perhaps mankind itself, may be about to make its last revolution unless some entirely new influence enters man's life as an active force.

So there I stand, week after week, lecturing to your colleagues in the role of someone who is supposed to represent the search for universal truth. And each week, without exception, it is I who turn away from questions dealing with the inner world of universal ideas. They, for their part, simply follow my lead. How could it be otherwise? If I steer the discussion to strictly pragmatic issues, how can I expect them to bring matters back to a deeper level of inquiry? I tell myself that I must not try to impose esoteric ideas on people who may not want to hear them. I tell myself that they themselves must step forward and ask for that sort of inquiry. And that is quite correct—they, you, must step forward in front of that interval. Such ideas must be asked for and cannot be forced on people. Yet, first these ideas must be made available and that is where I experience my own failure of nerve.

I wish now to tell you exactly what I tried in the most recent sequence of four seminars. Take it as a kind of confession on my part, but understand, please, that I write to you in this way and at such length in an effort to call forth from you something that I have not succeeded in calling forth from your colleagues.

Each seminar was devoted to a specific topic, as follows:

1. *To Whom Is the Physician Responsible?*
2. *The Art of Living and the Art of Medicine*

3. *Care*

4. *The Financial Disease of Modern Medicine*

In each case, I provided an advance "statement of the issues" in which I sought to suggest a bridge between the pragmatic problems of the practice of medicine and the indestructible questions of man's very life on earth.

Stay with me, doctor.

9. To Whom Is the Physician Responsible?

STATEMENT OF THE ISSUES

How can physicians find their way amid the conflicting responsiblities thrust upon them by the complexities of contemporary medical practice? Under what conditions does the obligation to care for the individual patient run counter to the physician's allegiance to the profession, the institution (or corporation) for which he works, or to a society characterized by limited resources? Is there a sense in which the physician's own personal limits of time and energy demand that he give primary responsibility to his own or his family's welfare?

Does the ideal of service to the suffering stand in need of redefinition? To what and for what is the individual physician of today really responsible?

Is the authority of the individual physican being eroded by the organizational changes of modern medical practice? If so, does this mean that the duties and responsibilities of the physician are correspondingly reduced? Who is really responsible for the care of the patient?

I requested that the above statement be distributed in advance throughout the hospital to all attending physicians, house staff, nurses, and administrators. My strategy, a wrong one as I now see, was to insert an inner question within the broad context of a well-recognized external problem—in this case, the whole problem of the conflicting allegiances under which so many physicians now suffer, a problem that, as I see from your letter, you too are struggling with.

Time was when doctors pursued their craft almost entirely on their own. There was no question about their responsibility. The well-being of the individual patient was the alpha and omega of their work. They gave orders to the patient—or, to be exact, they communicated to the patient in a form most likely to lend the patient will and hope and the strength of concentrated attention to his own organic well-being. I am speaking of good doctors, of course, not fools or charlatans, of which there have always been many. The good doctor instinctively understood why he must assume this position of total authority. He understood instinctively that this was an authority granted him by what used to be called "God," and which was later weakly translated as "compassion," and the meaning of which in our time has been almost completely destroyed through such words as *health care*. But let me reserve until later a discussion of the degeneration of the language of doctors.

Nowadays, the only patients who discover will-power in themselves are those who, through mere chance or through their own exceptional character development, see with objective horror both their own situation and the total helplessness of their doctors, and, having no taste whatever for self-deception, find that there is no place to go but "up"—that is, inside themselves, where they chance to find the existence of a truly higher psychophysical energy that carries them through either what is called a "miraculous" cure or an honorable death.

The good doctors of former times understood, instinctively, that they could assist the activation and concentration of this special force in their patients through the manner in which the doctor took responsibility. They saw, perhaps unconsciously, that it was in this that their patients needed most help because, in their physically weakened state, their patients could not even begin to call on their own special energy of concentrated attention.

The development of modern medical technology enabled doctors to treat only those illnesses whose cure did not require this special individual force from the mind and the heart of the patient. In this, modern medicine soared far beyond ancient medicine until now there is a complete failure to see the difference between these two kinds of illnesses—one that requires inner psychic power on the part of the sick person and the other that is mainly a mechanical disturbance needing mechanical repair. And where this distinction is once again being discussed, under the names of "patient responsibility" and "placebo effect," there is no clear distinction between encouraging in the patient the fantasy of inner will and the reality of inner will, not to mention cases where through charlatanistic impulses or sheer stupidity, the doctor or "practitioner" encourages fantasy just where physicomechanical means are necessary, and vice versa. In short, the entire issue has been confused by the term "psychosomatic," because the part of the human psyche that is most centrally involved in the cure of illness, namely the attention or will, is not understood in the contemporary era.

Among ancient systems of medicine, one finds indications of a profound and perhaps even conscious, scientific understanding of this psychic force. But only when this force is clearly understood and properly evaluated in oneself will it be possible to see where it was employed in the medical traditions of other cultures. Therefore, the study of ancient systems of medicine by itself can yield relatively little help in bringing this inner force into play in contemporary medicine. For this, the doctor himself, in his own individual being, has to experience and correctly value this energy, which means the doctor himself has to work on himself from a psychospiritual point of view, as was apparently the case in the training of physicians in other times and places, such as ancient India and China, and perhaps in the monasteries of early medieval Europe.

But the principal misunderstanding, which opens the door to all the others, is the false assumption that when the doctor is authoritative, it necessarily breeds mere passivity on the part of the patient. Modern man in general does not understand, it seems, that the forceful, authentic exercise of authority actually helps to strengthen the will of those upon whom this authority is exercised. The explanation of this is as follows: The power of *will* in man is only understandable as the lower functions obeying the higher within the individual. As the ancient Stoics realized—and in this they were following a vastly more ancient and comprehensive system of psychology—the true individual self of a man is something like a holographic mirror of the entire cosmic order. Slumbering in the essence of the individual human being are the great, active universal laws of the whole of creation. The Hebrews called this slumbering greatness "I AM." Authority in its authentic sense exists between people when one of them, who has perfected himself to the point where these laws are actively awake in his own being, helps another to find within himself the action of these same universally good and creative laws. Authority, in a word, is a demand made by the higher nature of one human being upon the lower nature of another human being, whereby the latter is called upon to obey and serve that in himself that this lower nature is meant to obey.

But enough of these metaphysical-psychological abstractions. The point is that the good doctors of former times understood instinctively that a physically ill person often needs great external help in order to find internal force within himself. The effect of the authentic exercise of authority is that the patient discovers that what is being demanded of him is something he *can* do, that there is something in himself he can trust beyond his fears and his emotionally compromised reasoning. That is to say, in illness all one's available psychic energy is being absorbed by bodily functions, and external help is often needed in order to free some of this energy for self-attention. Will in man is nothing if it is not free psychic energy.

I have repeatedly characterized the exercise of personal authority by the good doctors of former times as "instinctive." It is perhaps not the best word. Perhaps "automatic" or "intuitive" in the popular sense of the word would have been better. What I am saying is that these good doctors could not have understood consciously and scientifically exactly why the assuming of responsibility and the exercise of personal authority was so important in so many of their cases. They simply occupied a role, which I believe was originally created by truly wise physician-sages of former epochs, such as perhaps those physicians in the school of the legendary Asclepius.

I feel this must be so in order to explain why contemporary

physicians are so ready to surrender this role, something which they recently began doing at first reluctantly and gradually, but which many of them are now doing wholesale and with great gusto.

It is true that they have grounds for surrendering this role. The modern era has become increasingly spellbound by false authority and can no longer distinguish authority from authoritarianism. The principal kind of authority that we have seen is that which exploits the passivity of people, which plays on their weak side. Under the influence of this kind of authority, people lose what little self-power they have, as has been most clearly and horribly evident in the big political crimes of the past century where whole nations surrendered themselves to the ravings of individual madmen. I would like sometime to discuss this planetary phenomenon further with you, to see if you agree that this mass surrender of individual self-power, or liberty, is in part due to the fact that modern people more and more have come to live by the mind alone, with less and less intentional contact between the head and the organic energies of feeling and organic sensation.

In any case, I see now how foolish I was to hope anything of all this would emerge in the discussions without my taking a more forceful role. Up to a point, my strategy was right. As a first step, I did want the audience to see the whole external context of the problem of physician responsiblity. And this did come out rather clearly. Everyone agreed that uncontrolled medical specialization had eroded the physician's sense of individual responsibility. No individual doctor could possibly believe he knew enough to treat most of his serious cases all by himself. He constantly must call on consultants, specialists. No one doctor could begin to master all the medical knowledge now available, nor feel comfortable in front of all the sophisticated technologies and pharmaceuticals constantly being developed.

To make matters worse, the ever-present threat of malpractice suits forces the doctor to bring in outside consultants even where he might otherwise wish to handle a case by himself. Should something go wrong in the treatment, there are always attorneys ready to accuse the doctor of irresponsibility in not availing himself of specialists.

In addition, medicine itself has become more and more an industry, with money in its modern form entering into every corner of the doctor-patient relationship, thereby bringing this relationship more and more under the sway of the crude, powerful forces that govern human beings in the mass. This aspect of modern medicine had to be brought out right at the start, although I tried to hold back special consideration of it because the problem of money is for contemporary people, the most elusive of all the central questions of living. There is simply no clear guidance about this question in any of the great philosophies of the past.

Nevertheless, it had to be pointed out that the industrialization and socialization of medicine was an inevitable concomitant of the development of sophisticated medical technology. The growing influence of medical insurance companies had also to be brought out.

In short, by the time the evening was over, only the most external meaning of the idea of physician responsibility had been discussed. We had not even come within shouting distance of the far more essential inner meaning of this question that I had tried to insert in the second paragraph of my "statement of the issues" with the formulation: "To what and for what is the individual physician of today really responsible?" I had hoped that someone would read this phrase as applying to the whole question of individual free will and moral obligation, thus providing me with a platform upon which to go into the deeper psychological implications of this issue. I had especially hoped I could dangle in front of the doctors the notion that no man can be responsible to another human being until he strives to awaken in himself an inner force that can take responsiblity for his own mental, emotional, and physical impulses. I am speaking of the ancient teaching that no man has the right or ability to be obeyed until he himself obeys that which is higher within himself. And I knew that if this idea were to be brought out in a simple and serious way, all the external political, social and legal issues would, at least in principle, dispose themselves in an entirely fresh and hopeful way. But nothing of this idea appeared.

10. The Art of Living and the Art of Medicine

Before going on to what happened at the second seminar, which bore this title, I must tell you that Arthur Patai telephoned me this morning. I knew him, of course, from his participation in the seminars, but I did not especially feel like dropping everything to have lunch with him. However, when he said that he had just been with you at a conference in Philadelphia and brought me your greetings, it was like a bolt of lightning and I immediately arranged to meet him at the hospital. I still haven't calmed down from that meeting.

Young Dr. Patai must have thought I was slightly mad the way I kept asking about you, especially what you look like now! But I have come away with a rather clear picture of you, much better than I would have gotten from a photograph. You know how it is. We really don't remember people very well apart from a few static images from the past. Only rarely, from down in our depths, does a moving image of someone appear from which we can sense the real life of a loved one. All real feelings have to do with people in movement. All the false emotions are connected with static images.

So at the risk of being thought slightly mad by you as well, let me tell you what you look like.

You are still a tall and commanding presence, although the stoop of you shoulders has become more pronounced. You are still strong—not athletic exactly, but solid, tough. Your dark hair has almost entirely receded and is now a frizzled crescent of salt-and-pepper gray. Your voice has become dry and is no longer the deep and sonorous instrument it once was.

You are constantly in motion. Even when you are standing

still, it seems that you are always about to move somewhere else. You want to take everything in quickly. This is not how you used to be.

Dr. Patai admiringly portrayed this trait of yours. He spoke of the time when he trained under you—how on training rounds you would move so quickly from patient to patient that none of the residents could keep up with you. Yet, he said, in thirty seconds you were able to grasp more about the patient's condition even than the resident who had been working the wards day and night.

I granted Dr. Patai everything. I have no doubt about your brilliance. But, I ask you, what exactly did you intend to teach by this?

Why, this young Dr. Patai is a nervous wreck! Did you mean to teach them haste? Can you imagine what you would have given them by taking longer with each patient than any of them?

But now it is I who am going ahead of myself. I only wanted to tell you about my meeting with Dr. Patai because it brought me one step closer to you, to actually seeing you again. And also, because you know him, you will be especially interested to hear about his participation in these seminars.

In the second seminar, I sent out the following:

STATEMENT OF THE ISSUES

The problem of "the impaired physician" is now a well-documented and well-labelled phenomenon. What is less clear is the extent to which the forces that produce this phenomenon are at work in the lives of all physicians. The "impaired physician" phenomenon compels us to ask about the interdependence of the quality of the physician's personal life and the quality of his or her practice of medicine. Can the destructive impulses of fear and egoism in one's personal life so easily be set aside as one undertakes the task of caring for patients? If not, then the age-old philosophical questions of right living become issues of intense practical relevance to every practicing physician. Or, are we prepared to say that scientific knowledge, advanced technology and "the tricks of the trade" are by themselves enough to ensure an acceptable level of medical competence?

To what extent and in what sense is being a good physician related to the question of being a good human being? In an era of rapid cultural change, when so many traditional outer forms of ethical behavior are problematic, is it necessary to seek an internal, psychological definition of *virtue* in one's personal and professional life?

I must say that even now, when I see the phrase *impaired physician*, it still brings a grudging smile to my lips. What a genius we have for labelling things! If only we could carry that genius over to our actual behavior! Under this term, *impaired physician*, are included the astonishing number of doctors who are alcoholics, drug addicts, and suicidally depressed. I have heard the term *wounded healer* applied to such people, but I think that term is best reserved for doctors who are themselves physically ill and who thereby discover real truths about the experience of illness in their patients. No, "impaired physician" is excellent. It's a term wholly without moralistic judgment, and yet it applies to what used to be understood as the moral weakness of man— the absence of will, the betrayal of ideals, the slavery to the emotions. Because of the fact that all doctors of whatever stripe understand through experience what their colleagues have to go through, they have hit upon a phrase that approaches authentic objectivity, an objectivity that is rooted in feeling and that is worlds apart from the so-called objectivity of most modern science. This latter so-called objectivity, which is often paraded forth as the crown jewel of the scientific attitude, has become little more than the heartless mechanism of the intellect buffered off from the feelings.

It seems to me that if physicians are looking for a model of how to be toward their patients, they could do worse than to take stock of how they are toward their own colleagues! There is an old Scottish saying that, I believe, goes something like this: "If you see someone behaving toward another with real compassion, you can be sure that he himself is on the cross."

My strategy, therefore, in this second seminar was to focus

attention at the outset on this easily recognized problem of the impaired physician. From this, we would move to the inescapable fact that everyone is more or less an "impaired" human being. The same forces that lead some people to suicide or drugs operate on all of us. The difference is only in the particular forms in which these forces manifest. And from this it is only a short step to the notion, which has been a guiding beacon of truth in all the great teachings of the past, that external factors are not the main reason that our actions fall so far short of what we desire. Our actions are what they are mainly because we are what we are.

Starting from this conclusion, as I intended, we could then look at the problem facing doctors without being trapped into blaming external conditions, but instead directing our inquiry to our own inner psychological states, which are the chief cause of all man's sorrows on this earth. For example, your young protégé, Dr. Patai. He has a strong ambition to help suffering people, but instead of making him open to the needs of others, this strong ambition merely makes him tense. But more about him later.

The next part of my plan was as follows. Having brought forward the all-important psychological dimension of the art of medicine, the stage would be set for the most essential and most difficult part of the inquiry. I had no doubt people would agree to the importance of psychology and might even agree that "impaired physicians" were not all that different from the rest of them. Where I expected to meet resistance was in proposing that the psychological concepts and methods with which they were all familiar were totally and irredeemably inadequate to the task of bringing them the self-knowledge they needed in order to become authentic physicians. I intended to suggest that the qualities of the good physician are inseparable from the qualities that make up the being of a real and authentic human being—namely, impartiality; impersonal love; inner freedom from opinion, fear, and tension; and the instinctive sensing of the manner in which nature actually operates in the body and the mind of man—with its concomitant power of balancing in oneself the impressions of reality that come from one's own genuine intuition and experience and the systematically organized information that one has acquired externally through education and intellectual study.

In anticipation of exploring this whole question, I had invited the head of the psychiatry division to be a member of the panel. I had readied myself to bring forward the views about Freud that I described to you in a previous letter—namely, that Freud had unconsciously discovered within himself the existence of a level and quality of human attention hitherto unsuspected and unrecognized by modern science, and that this force of attention had not only served to balance Freud's own intellectual and emotional functions, thereby enabling him to be compassionate and insightful in the presence of his patients, but also that this force of attention itself "radiated" to his patients a really effective healing influence, both in the sense of tangible healing energy and in the sense of calling forth in them the arising of their own self-mobilizing power of inner attention. I should add that I was also prepared to speculate out loud about somatic healing procedures in other cultures and other times in the light of this idea about the ruling energy of attention that Freud had stumbled upon. This would have provided, I think, an interesting context in which to attempt to discriminate the pearl of value amid the fantasies that have originated in California under the name of "holistic medicine."

The point here would have been to suggest that in certain ancient cultures there existed a greater or lesser conscious understanding of the energy of attention in man and that patterns of life in these cultures were formed on the basis of this understanding. For example, the laws of the ancient Hebrews, as written down in the books of Moses, provide clues to the existence of this understanding. And since this all-important factor of levels of attention in the human psyche long ago ceased to be recognized by modern man, the rituals and patterns of living laid down by Moses—and in other "orthodoxies"—became incomprehensible and were gradually dissolved by the acids of egoistic intellectualism under the name of "modernization." The inner struggle necessary to manufacture the higher level of attention disappeared from our culture. The aim of life became comfort—first physical and then psychological comfort. But as the wise men and women of the past knew, it is not in the cards for man to become both comfortable and conscious at the same time. And since it is impossible for man to live well without being under the inner rule of his own authentic conscious attention, the life of modern man became metaphysically wretched to the precise extent that it was oriented solely toward psychophysical comfort.

Of course, I did not expect the seminar to reach this level of inquiry. I hoped only to suggest that to become a real doctor, it is necessary to strive to become a real man. For this, it is first of all necessary to see how far one really is from this goal and to see it in a way that produces a self-transformative inner suffering—in a word, to awaken conscience, rather than guilt. And I ask you, what doctor has not had moments of this in front of his limitations in the face of his patient's mortality? What doctor has not had moments of seeing himself against the vast metaphysical scale of the sorrow inherent in that little lump of mortal spit and clay called man—man, whose awareness of the fact of his own inevitable death is the only intimation he has of a deeper order of reality?

In a word, both real compassion and real intuitive knowledge are functions of conscious attention, without which scientific information and altruistic emotions are blind. And who but the physician, in our society, has the chance to enter so deeply into the sufferings of mankind that, if he but direct his attention on himself in the process, it is all but guaranteed that his power of seeing will at times begin to emanate from that level of mind that our ancient teachers called "the inner divinity" and that I myself have learned to call real attention? For it is one thing to notice and be unsettled by people's miserableness; it is another to encounter with the full weight of mind the lawful misery of infinite man in his finite body, to be offered the details of that misery, and to be privileged with the obligation of helping him in some real way or other. Such a vocation will, without any doubt, either make or break a man. Thus the physician is either the best or the worst of men, for what is more to be pitied or despised than a bad physician? Doctor, you have no choice. You had better be a good man or you will end by becoming the worst of men. I am saying that your vocation offers you almost all you need to become good—and therefore intelligent and effective in your practice. *"Almost"*: the rest of what you need is up to people like me to offer you, people like me who have come across great universal ideas about the human condition and who are obliged to try to hand them on to others who actually live and work in the day-to-day life of the world.

But what can I do? My two panelists, one of whom was the psychiatrist I have mentioned, played their parts well enough and spoke to the question quite sincerely. My psychiatrist painted a vivid picture of the pressures and responsibilities that weigh so heavily on the doctors, and my other panelist, a highly respected administrative physician, spoke insightfully and with wry humor about the disillusionments inherent in the contemporary practice of medicine. But I could not shoehorn in a single indication that the role of physician demands the development of the doctor's inner being, rather than merely the repair of his ego—or, in the words of the great Paracelsus, "The art of medicine is rooted in the heart. If your heart is false, you will also be a false physician; if your heart is just, you will also be a true physician," and again, "The physician should be a whole man in the sense that his mind is free," or, according to an even more venerable source, "My true sons and pupils are those who can preserve the lives of others because they have died to themselves."

In other words, I was not able to trail my garment. In fact, when I tried to do so, it was your student, Dr. Patai, who jumped on it with muddy feet. Here is what happened:

When the panelists had finished their opening presentations, the following picture of the contemporary physician had emerged:

The doctor of today, man or woman, has lost every possibility of a normal family life. He is almost never at home, and when he is at home, he is tired and drained. His children never see him. His spouse becomes lonely and despondent.

The doctor of today is no longer an individual meeting another individual who needs him. Instead, he is a cog in a machine, a pawn, a plaything of forces within the colossal, multibillion dollar "health-care industry." He has been stripped of all power, while at the same time he is still held legally and morally responsible for the welfare of his patients. This condition of responsibility without actual power breeds a swarm of neuroses, self-deceptions, tensions and unbearable guilt feelings, especially in that large majority of doctors who are, as personality types, what might be termed "overachievers."

Because of advanced technology, and because of the godlike image that the public has thrust upon him and that he has willingly accepted, the doctor of today is the focus of unrealistic expectations, which increase the above-mentioned unbearable guilt-feelings.

The doctor of today is not free to practice the art of medicine. The intangibles of personal relationship, intuitive experimentation, and that special quality of inspired patience and watchfulness in treatment have been taken away from him. There are always lawyers breathing down his neck ready to sue him for failing to follow "acceptable" modes of treatment that are often actually inappropriate or unnecessary in a particular case. He lives in dread of lawyers.

The doctor of today is therefore either riddled with tension or stuffed with complacency. But above and beyond this, he is bored. He is nervous and bored, or he is complacent and bored. But he *is* bored. Surrounded by fantastic technology and sophisticated research data, he nevertheless finds himself droning through the same routines day in and day out, or masking this essential boredom with feverish activity or countless distractions. Three-quarters of his patients are not even really sick, but only worried. And this is not to mention those who come to him only for purposes of legitimizing some trumped-up insurance claim.

It was when this subject of boredom came up that I saw my chance to introduce transpsychological ideas into the discussion, even though I saw that your Dr. Patai, sitting in the front row, was already bursting to say something.

"Excuse me," I began, "but of all the factors you have enumerated that make up the desolate life of the contemporary physician, I think boredom is the most important. I realize that modern psychiatry has not considered this phenomenon of basic importance and I understand why. But speaking from the perspective of my own specialty, philosophy, I would have to say that boredom is the central disease of modern man. I see boredom as a disease of the knowing function of mind, that function which psychiatry had almost entirely neglected—as is evidenced by its failure to consider the role of ideas in the psychological development of normal human beings.

"As I have come to understand it," I went on, "the psychophysical integrity of the human being is so constructed that the constant assimilation of knowledge is necessary even for its biological life to proceed properly. The physical body of man itself requires what could be called the food, or energy, or even the *matter* of knowledge.

"In part, this disease is the result of the poor quality of ideas with which modern man has surrounded himself. The concepts of modern science are applicable only to a restricted segment of life and so anything that falls outside that segment is no longer encountered with the mind. And since the mind is the seat of the sense of self, at least for us modern people, most of the events of our lives pass by without being actively encountered by the sensation and feeling of *I am*. When *I am* exists in the human presence, then and only then is all of life passionately interesting.

"Boredom is the emotion that informs us that there is no feeling of *I am* in our presence . . . "

I intended to continue by pointing out that since man cannot exist without the feeling of self-identity, the psychological vacuum of boredom simply must be filled, if not by an authentic experience of *I am*, then by a counterfeit experience. That is to say, external stimulation of the senses or the activation of previously engraved emotional impressions takes place by necessity in the absence of the true experience of self-presence. Or, to put the point in more common language, people crave external simulation of any kind simply in order to feel they exist. Or, again, in the words of Pascal, "all the unhappiness of men arises from one single fact, that they cannot stay quietly in their own chamber."

Since I was unable to say these things there, allow me to tell you, briefly, where this line of thought leads. The point is that the authentic self of man has all the attributes needed for an individual not only to be a good doctor but to be a good man even in this present cultural environment. But this authentic self is not born out of nothing. It must be cultivated and nurtured very carefully and over a long period of time. This cultivation takes place through the development of self-attention in the mind, feelings, and physical sensation. The embryo of this authentic self is a sincere, that is to say, objective and precise effort to be aware and attentive to one's own inner impressions in the midst of one's ordinary, everyday activity. Even this embryonic self-attention has remarkable power as a moral influence, but only—as has been told in countless fairytales—if one's "heart" is pure, that is, only if one's motivation is to be aware of the truth, no matter what it is. And in order to bring attention to oneself, one needs to begin with ideas about the structure of man and the world that can accurately guide and direct this embryonic self-study, ideas that are not limited to the observation of one segment of the external world. In a word, self-observation, rightly conducted, is the seed of the the appearance of *I am*, which alone makes man human. You will recall that when Moses brought the laws of right living to the people of Israel, he was given to understand that the source of all power and wisdom was named *"I am."*

I don't think that your protégé, Dr. Patai, was aware that he was interrupting anything. On the contrary, he obviously felt that he had the answer to all the problems we were raising when he jumped up and began discoursing about the need to redefine the doctor-patient relationship along the lines of a contract between two equally responsible parties.

He made frequent use of the phrase, *medical paternalism*, to characterize what was wrong with the doctor-patient relationship and what needed to be corrected. For too long, he said, doctors have presumed to make judgments that are, strictly speaking, beyond their proper sphere of competence and training, interfering with the patient's liberty and autonomy under the alleged justification that this interference is in the best interests of the patient. For too long doctors have been inclined to withhold information from their patients or make decisions about treatment without seeking the patient's informed consent. "This," said Dr. Patai, "not only violates the moral rights of the patient, but is also completely unjustified by the latest scientific, clinical evidence."

Although he was looking at the audience as he spoke, I soon realized he was really addressing his remarks to me as a representative of the public. He went on, starting slowly and then increasing the tempo and volume of his voice:

"We physicians," he said, "would gladly continue to shoulder the personal burdens on our lives that have been described by Dr.——(here he mentioned the psychiatrist on the platform) if there were good evidence that assuming such overwhelming responsibilities were in the best interests of our patients. I will go further and say that were such evidence forthcoming, then I, like every doctor here, would run to embrace even more responsibilities and burdens than we now suffer under.

"But there is no such evidence. Quite the contrary. And therefore we physicians must insist on doing our patients the honor of regarding them as free and equal human beings who, no less than we ourselves, have the right and power to make their own decisions and assume responsibility and obligations just like the rest of humanity.

"Of course," he continued, "if I were one morning to wake up and find myself possessed with the miraculous power of reading minds or if, like the great lawgiver Moses whom our distinguished philosopher is so fond of quoting, I were suddenly visited by God and chosen to be the divinely appointed arbiter of moral judgment for all mankind and, in addition, were gifted with the faculty of seeing into the future, then I would not hesitate to regard my patients as children and not only make their medical decisions for them, but their personal and ethical decisions as well.

"Until that happy day arrives, however, I will go on regarding myself and my patients as equals. I have a specific technical training and expertise that, for a fair price, I place at the disposal of my patient. He or she, as a free and autonomous being, willingly undertakes to accept or reject my services. If he or she accepts them, then he or she must also undertake the responsibilities that go with them—namely, to obey my instructions, and not to expect from me more than I have contracted to deliver to him or her, such as miraculous healing powers or other manifestations of sainthood."

At this point, Dr. Patai noticed, I think, that he was entirely caught up in the momentum of his speech. He paused for a moment and collected himself, and then went on in softer tones:

"It is my concern for the dignity and autonomy of the patient that dictates that we treat the physician-patient relationship as a legal contract, rather than as a divinely inspired covenant. In former times, doctors had little more to offer their patients than the illusion of godlike wisdom and power. The physician of former times was little more than a walking and talking placebo. But now we actually have technical power—power undreamt of in former times. And this finally enables us to elevate the patient to the status of an adult human being and, at the same time, enables us to live our own lives as normal human beings without trying to conform to the abnormal pretensions of sainthood. Give me time and space, and you will find me as compassionate and caring as can be expected of any normal human being. Let me lead a decent and well-ordered life and you will find me to be a decent and sensitive dispenser of health care. But thrust upon me unrealistic personal demands and pathogenic psychological pressures and insist that I demean the freedom and autonomy of my patients and I will soon not only be included in the ranks of the impaired physicians, but my patients will suffer harm to their bodies and their souls."

With this, your protégé, Dr. Patai, concluded his remarks and sat down. The audience murmured for a moment and expressed its approval with a modest ripple of applause.

Had I known then what was to take place in the subsequent seminars, I would certainly not have felt quite so dismayed by Dr. Patai's speech, which, for all its hypocrisy, still acknowledged—if only to deny—the idea of a possible higher source of authority within himself. That he acknowledged this idea at all I attributed to the influence of your personal being upon his unconscious feelings—but, of course, you never gave him any concepts about the world that could support those feelings in his work and make them an active force in his mind.

As I say, had I known what was to come later, I would not have been so cast down. But in Dr. Patai's remarks I saw for the first time the immensity of the forces that are acting upon doctors in the present era. The metaphysician in me rose up with the sensation that, yes, this has all happened before countless times in human history. There is nothing new under the sun. In this tiny microcosm of the medical profession, were we not witnessing the same play of forces that on a far larger scale had countless times in the past led to the destruction of higher values in the life of mankind? A noble idea, such as human freedom and dignity, becomes detached from an all-around understanding of the complexities of life and surreptitiously attaches itself to a human weakness, such as the desire for comfort or pleasure or recognition and not only masks these weaknesses, but reinforces them with that special human energy that, under the right conditions, is actually the impulse that can lead man to the struggle for real knowledge and inner moral growth. On the great stage of human history, has not this dialectic played itself out countless times and under countless names which now read like the names of rivers of blood—"altruism," "equality," "fraternity," "liberty"?

Of course, this "revolution" in the practice of medicine is not proceeding through violence and murder, as have the revolutions in the history of nations. But the result in this relatively little world is the same: the attainment of certain temporary material advantages at the cost of those qualities of conscious human experience without which even prolonged human life, assuming for a moment that it really can be attained apart from the context of such experiences, is as hollow and desolate as the life of an ant colony.

I see the role of the physician as though it were some necessary life form within the strictly human "ecosystem." Destroy this life form, this ontologically predetermined role in the total life of mankind, and you have removed from human life an irreplaceable "creature" upon whom many other forms of human life and experience depend.

I confess that I spent much of the remainder of the seminar lost in thought about this force in the affairs of men that has acted as a levelling principle throughout human history. Civilization has existed for a long time even though this downward force has always been present, as it must. Then, there must also always exist a counterforce, moving toward the refinement and harmonization of the whole life of man. Were it otherwise, human civilization would have long since perished. But what is this movement of authentic renewal? It cannot be a mass movement. There is no mass movement in all of history that carries this upward force. Study any book of history and there you will find only the record of the downward force in one or another of its stages, and often in its final stages that are marked by violence, crime and war. The "great events" of history are merely the crimes that have happened to attract our attention.

This upward force must exist, by necessity. But it cannot be seen where we look for it. The conclusion is clear. It proceeds only within the interior life of individuals striving to be and to live according to the eternally new and unknown immense potentialities of knowledge and love hidden within the structure of human nature.

After Dr. Patai took his seat, a heated discussion took place round about his "contractual theory" of medical ethics. I will send you a transcript.

11. Care

The secret of caring for the patient is caring for the patient.

—OSLER

The problem to be addressed in tonight's symposium is as simple to state as it is difficult to answer: How to care?—not as an abstract attitude, but in the day-to-day realities of the practice of medicine. Associated with this "simple" question are all the emotional stresses and difficulties of being a physician. Is it possible, in the contemporary milieu, for the practice of medicine, conceived as the art of helping the suffering, to be intrinsically rewarding, apart from material gain and social recognition?

I don't know what Dr. Patai told you about this next seminar on the subject of care. It is true that I suddenly changed my plans and invited him to be the principal panelist, but it was not because I was hunting for some kind of confrontation with him, although I suspect that is what he must have believed by the end of the evening. The simple fact is that, for all his wiseacring about the so-called rights of the patient, there is something about him that touches me very deeply. Something in his eyes, like the look of a young animal or an innocent child. His opinions about the rights of the patient, no matter how emotionally he held them, did not penetrate down to his inner depths—this I felt. As I have said, such opinions, so logical and so decent at their level, actually prevent an individual from reaching toward what is authentically higher in himself. They freeze man at a level of thought and feeling, and hence at a level of action, which is subhuman, superficially rational and ethical. They persuade man to stay at his present level, of this I am now certain.

The issue here goes beyond the question of how to be a real

physician, important though this is in itself. In fact, the issue is nothing less than: "What is the work of man, a real man, or someone seeking to be a real man?" It is true that the practice of medicine, like everything else in modern life, is changing so rapidly that the old ideals no longer can be applied in the old ways. But to me all that means is that we must search without respite for the essence of the work of man in these new outer conditions. This work must be found and it can be found. But it is difficult.

And one of the chief elements in this difficulty is attachment to our opinions. Dr. Patai interested me—no, *interest* is not the right word. He *drew* me to him because there so clearly exists in him an unspoiled wish for truth side by side with an extremely strong resistance to it in the form of attachment to logically reasoned ethical opinions that are based on a profound underestimation of man's possible evolution and a complete ignorance of the way an individual must work for this evolution in the midst of his station in life. His eyes yearn for Being and in equal measure his automatic mind and emotions draw him away from it. I long ago realized that I cannot help but feel love for such a person.

I had originally entitled the seminar "Care vs. Cure" in order to point up the obvious problems associated with the great technological successes of modern medicine. As I stated it in my opening remarks, the contemporary physician is trained only to cure and receives almost no preparation for the task of caring. He is geared to fix problems and repair damage. But he is becoming more and more helpless in front of the whole range of his patient's emotional needs that in their way are of utmost importance to the patient's recovery.

And with the large percentage of patients with chronic illnesses who will never be completely well, the physician geared mainly to curing increasingly turns away from his proper role. Finally, patients with terminal illnesses are often simply abandoned in one way or another.

There was little for anyone to object to in these opening remarks of mine. I limited myself to speaking only about the emotional needs of the patient and did not even mention the metaphysical needs. I was hoping that sometime late in the discussion I could bring in this point, which I can state quite openly to you, doctor, but which I was not sure how to bring into the context of the seminar.

To you I can be direct about this—isn't that so? You *do* understand what I am asking about—don't you? I don't particularly like the term *metaphysical* in speaking about these needs, but it is the best I can think of, wishing at all costs to avoid words that would suggest anything religious in the customary sense of that term, as in our era religion has more or less descended to the level of the therapeutic, understood as the art of putting pleasant dreams in the place of unpleasant dreams.

The question has nothing to do with religion in this sense. It has to do with freeing oneself from all dreams, pleasant and unpleasant, including the dream of life itself. Do you still care for your patients in that way, doctor? While attending to your patients' physical health and emotional needs, do you increase or decrease their illusions and attachments? Do you help them to become still, or do you merely tranquilize them? Do they leave your care more of a slave to the body and its vicissitudes, or less of a slave? In short, are you an awakening or a dormitive influence upon them?

A patient is, almost by definition, someone who is to some degree confronted with the question of his own life, his own self. Almost by definition, his suffering is to some degree a mode of confronting the unconscious psychophysical habits with which we identify throughout our lives. What kind of an influence are you in the life of this patient? That is what these letters to you are about. It is the only question I am asking. It defines the place you hold in my memory. It is what you were to me when I was a young child. Your presence, your attention, your impersonal love for something in me that was higher and more intimate to me than my frightened ego is what remains in my memory of you. While caring for my body, you were also a kind of extraordinary educator siding with that in me that yearned for inner freedom, inner being. And I repeat what I wrote in my first letters: It was not what you said, it was what you were. You were my first real teacher. You helped me to touch that deeply natural place in the heart that is free of pain and pleasure. You did not comfort me in a way that chained me further to my imagination and fears. You showed me the world of men.

Are we to accept that it is no longer possible for a doctor to work like this and have this kind of influence in the life of his patients? Why? Because medicine is now organized too much like a corporate business? But all our lives are being swept into the process of corporate-computer rationalization. Is it because of the power of new technologies that undermine the physician's trust in his own reason and intuition? But technology is entering into the intimate decision of everyone's life, not just yours. Is it because of government, money, lawyers, paperwork? That is everyone's life, doctor, not just yours. If we are to accept that you cannot work like a man, then none of us can. I don't accept that.

But read on.

12. Technology

In addition to Dr. Patai, who epitomized the new formation of the idea of the doctor-patient relationship, my other panelist was a nephrologist, Dr. Gilbert Bloom, with many years of experience conducting and supervising the treatment of patients requiring kidney dialysis. He was my representative of technology—the good and the bad of it. I will tell you about Dr. Bloom a little later, as it was in him that I saw my first ray of hope for the future of medicine.

Knowing that the subject of advanced medical technology would form an important part of the seminar—as it had in all the previous discussions—I decided to prepare myself by witnessing firsthand an example of the achievement of medical technology. I asked for and was immediately granted permission to watch open-heart surgery.

I was just a little bit unsettled by the ease with which permission was granted, but I chalked that up to my own old-fashioned and outdated opinions and images about surgery as some dangerous, difficult, and even arcane crisis-laden event requiring the utmost in intensity of concentration and emotional containment conducted in an atmosphere of silence bordering on spiritual devotion. This picture of medicine as a kind of initiatic discipline is, I freely admit, romantic. But as a symbol of the conditions under which the real work of man must proceed, it is accurate enough and I do not intend to let go of it.

I arrived in the early morning, as instructed, and was directed to the doctors' locker room where I was provided with a surgical cap, mask, and sterile blue paper clothes. After slipping into these clothes, I proceeded through the halls following the OR signs and arrows, and then down two flights of stairs to a door that I presumed opened into the spectators' gallery.

When I opened the door, however, I found myself in the ante-chamber of the operating room. The spectators' gallery was above me. Evidently, I was to watch the procedure at much closer hand than I had imagined. This definitely intrigued me. I had assumed I would be at some remove from the surgery, for the fact was that, although I had considerable experience on postoperative recovery wards and had personally ferried practically every possible detached part of the human body, and although I had personally "operated" on many, many thoroughly dead bodies, I had never actually witnessed major surgery performed on a living person. I was definitely intrigued—and nervous.

Only then did I notice a naked human body spread out amid all the gleaming metal, dials, rubber hoses, monitor screens, and blue sheeting of the operating table. It startled me. I saw large areas of pinkish-gray—definitely the skin of a living human being. I made out a leg—two legs. And there was an arm and a breast— it was an elderly woman. But—hoses, dials, sheets—where was the head?

And suddenly, I saw the woman's head and face as I walked around the operating table. I have dissected many dead bodies and have seen numerous unconscious patients, but I had never seen a face in quite that state of unconsciousness. I've since been told that all deeply anesthetized patients have the same appearance. Maybe so. But there was something astonishing in it for me—the same astonishment we sometimes feel as children when for the first time we see, really see, someone asleep. This some-one—maybe it's one's mother or father—is alive, but the person is absent. The person—what is that? I remember feeling this once when watching my father sleep, his face utterly slack—I remember thinking something like: "No one should ever be that absent!"

In any case, I did not have time to pursue these strange and perhaps foolish thoughts. A squad of eight blue-clad men and women briskly entered the room and began taking charge. Feeling like an intruder, I modestly stepped away from the patient but was motioned back by the tallest member of the squad.

Everyone, of course, wore surgical masks and from that point on, I was relating to eyes, voices, and postures, rather than to faces. I should note here, without trying to make too much of it, the impression I had after the operation when the surgeon and the anesthesiologist removed their masks and we had a few minutes to talk together. I will only say that, having gotten to know them without faces, I at first found their faces strangely irrelevant. To tell the truth, they—including perhaps myself as well—were much more interesting without their faces. As I say, I do not want to make too much of this now, but remind me to speak to you further about this sometime. It has to do with the whole question of our personality or social self and how disconnected it is from what we actually are and do under the surface in our essential being. I cannot resist observing, however, that the face, or personal ego, of the surgeon, Dr. Ballentyne, was completely bewildered by what his essence loved to do simply for its own sake—namely, to pay close physical attention with a free and very concentrated mind, and a relatively relaxed body, to a physical-technical problem such as sewing two coronary blood vessels together.

I will come back to speaking about the personality of Dr. Ballentyne, which, thank God, was relatively free of missionary idealism, and will only mention here that during our interview he admitted that he earned more money than anyone really has a right to earn. Thank God for that, too. May he go on earning great sums of money! May he and those like him remain absolutely free to do what they love to do and do so well—namely, solve physical-technical problems with a joy and freedom that comes from deep down in their own essential nature. But I am getting ahead of myself, because my point here is to show just what it is that makes American medicine so extraordinarily good even as American physicians are rapidly becoming so extraordinarily bad.

I was motioned out of my corner by the anesthesiologist, Dr. Warenke, who positioned me right next to him. He sat himself atop a tall stool, commanding a number of monitors and several tubes leading into the patient's body. He explained that he could with great precision control the amount and kind of anesthesia simply by injecting the necessary substances into the intubation portals right in front of him. From where he sat, he could clearly observe the physiological and neuroelectric monitors, as well as study the patient's face that, from where he sat, was positioned at the level of his knees.

The surgical technician had already started the heart-lung machine, and the patient's blood was now being circulated and aerated through the machine that from the outside resembled a spotlessly white, mobile industrial vacuum cleaner. This technician, seeing my interest in his machine, came to my side and answered my questions about it. Then, having satisfied my curiosity, he jauntily skipped back to the machine and tapped a few of the dials.

The atmosphere in the room was very interesting. It was silent but not oppressive. Everyone was doing his proper job while retaining a quiet awareness of everyone else. The overall tempo was rapid but not rushed.

I asked Dr. Warenke the patient's name.

"Mildred Palmer," he said.

"Mrs.?" I asked.

He nodded yes.

I looked down at the infinitely unconscious face of Mrs. Palmer. "You seem to be in good hands, Mrs. Palmer," I whispered to her. Dr. Warenke smiled at that and continued turning knobs. It was when he started whistling a little popular tune that I started to become aware of the chief characteristic of this whole procedure and, indeed, of much of modern medicine itself.

All this, while the chief surgeon, Dr. Ballentyne, had been maintaining a running conversation with the nurses and with his assistant surgeon who was positioned across from him. Dr. Ballentyne's eyes looked at me, radiating, as I felt, warmth and energy.

He then began the incision on Mrs. Palmer's chest. I moved closer to him, my head swimming with primitive excitement. I kept telling myself that I was investigating modern medicine. But the truth was that I was also living out part of an old, deep dream—a dream of knowledge and of participation in the secrets of nature itself, God himself. Why beat around the bush? That is the simple truth.

I watched the thin red line of blood form under Dr. Ballentyne's scalpel and I caught my breath as he picked up the surgical saw and began cutting through the sternum. There was no longer any "Mrs. Palmer." There was only a sternum and under it the living human heart.

Dr. Ballentyne's hands were sure and deft, no wasted motion. In practically no time, the sternum was longitudinally severed and the gleaming metal brace inserted in order to spread the two halves of the breastbone apart.

I was struck, as always I have been, by the absolute mechanicalness of the human body. A clamp, a brace, a needle and thread, a knife—and there it lies in all its parts: the human body, sacred, awesome, the vehicle of mystery, consciousness and life. But however simple it looked, it took all the centuries and attention of mankind's best minds to cut and pull apart the body in this way.

And now suddenly there was the beating human heart less than eighteen inches from me.

I confess I very nearly wept.

Fortunately, there was no danger of anyone's noticing the state I was in. I could feel my eyes bulging as I bent forward to watch the heart in action. I wanted to touch it. I thought of ancient civilizations and the meaning of the heart as the center of life, the seat of the soul, the ultimate mystery and wonder. Seeing it now, a muscle the size of a fist, throbbing under its own mysterious source of power—actually seeing the heart in front of me. Not only did it lose none of its meaning; on the contrary, it seemed to me more extraordinary than ever. It was real, it was a material entity, not just a symbol. Again and again, I have experienced what it means to see a material reality: how the material realities of the world are full of immense truth and mind—so long as they are stripped of interpretation and sentiment, as they are stripped by the techniques of modern science.

A crushed ice solution was poured over the heart in order to render it inert. The patient's blood began to be diverted through the heart-lung machine and Dr. Ballentyne began examining the coronary arteries that supply the walls of the heart itself. Meanwhile, the assistant surgeon had moved to the other end of the table and was stripping out a vein from the patient's leg. This vein would be used by Dr. Ballentyne in repairing the coronary vessels.

Holding the inert heart with his hand, Dr. Ballentyne shook his head knowingly and then looked up at the rest of us. "Just about what we thought," he said, quite matter-of-factly, without a trace of optimism or pessimism in his voice. But although there was nothing in his voice to indicate a feeling of hope or promise for the patient, the moment his hands began to do their work, the situation was completely different. The room became charged with energy of a very definite sort, energy and movement of a very definite and familiar sort. Dr. Ballentyne's hands began to move, his fingers, his arms, the motions of his head and shoulders—all strong, clear, free—very free, very easy and extremely *relaxed*.

And Dr. Warenke, the anesthesiologist, continued to whistle.

What was going on here?

Dr. Ballentyne himself, although he did not whistle, did banter with the rest of us as his hands deftly sewed patches in the arteries of Mrs. Palmer's heart.

I looked again at the heart and again nearly wept as the sense of wonder surged through me.

And just then, by association, I remembered the feeling that I experienced some fourteen years ago looking at my television screen. Something very much like the living human heart was there on the screen—small, mysterious, incredibly real and powerful: the planet earth.

Mankind was seeing what it had never seen before, what had been a mystery and a symbol, but that now was a simple material reality, revealed to us by—by what? By scientific technology. Was there any mind at NASA or was there any scientist in the space program whose being or personal presence was equal to this phenomenal event of seeing the planet earth in space? No. They were all just smart scientists—no more, no less. And they whistled, too.

But more than that, there were these astronauts. How well they moved, how at home with machinery and technology, with calculations of dazzling complexity. How relaxed they were, how at home in their bodies. And when a malfunction occurred, when something blew out or chipped off that might mean their own death—yes, of course, they were afraid, but they moved without panic through it all. They whistled; while walking in interplanetary space—they whistled. Looking at planet earth, floating out of the gravity of earth, circling the moon, they joked and whistled.

In front of this living human heart, I recalled looking at the planet earth in space. And I felt the same presence around me as I had felt with respect to the astronauts. Dr. Ballentyne was an astronaut and so was Dr. Warenke and the whole team around me. I began to understand the American-ness of scientific technology and its connection to that aspect of the human mind that moves, acts, and "does."

In myself, in ourselves, there is a mind that moves the body, which quickly and automatically learns all the physcial movements of the physical body. One sees this mind and its power much more clearly in the animal world, but it is very much part of ourselves as well. For example, the phenomenon of "imprinting" in ethology is a clear example of that mind that quickly and without deviation learns the most complex series of physical postures and motions, enabling it to function in the natural world. Very many things in ourselves operate by means of this quality of mind—many of our skills, almost all of our physical behavior, even our talking and thinking, is governed by this moving mind or autonomic nervous system.

When it is said that modern technology is an extension of man's mind, it should be remembered that it is this moving-autonomic mind that is being spoken of. And those who are most at home with this quality of mind are often those men and women who are most at home in the world of physical action and scientific technology. They are centered in their body mechanisms and are sometimes very open to the logical mind as well, which, after all, is only the intellect in its mechanically functioning mode, the intellect as a machine, a filing system, a computer.

Just when I was having these thoughts, an event occurred that served to confirm them. The apparatus monitoring the patient's blood pressure and respiratory rate stopped functioning. I knew full well how essential it was to have a constant and accurate readout of this data—had I not just been shown how precisely calibrated these new anesthesiological methods had become and how the slightest miscue or failure of attention could mean death for the patient?

"The monitors are out," said Dr. Warenke, almost casually, while he eased himself off his high stool by the patient's head. Dr. Ballentyne seemed unconcerned and went on with his cutting and sewing as if nothing was wrong. The level of tension in the room was less than what one experiences when the toaster fails to work. "The outlets are okay," said the heart-lung machine attendant from the other end of the room.

"Better get it working," said Dr. Ballentyne softly. "Her pressure seems to be going down."

Dr. Warenke stood by his stool staring at the blank screens of the monitoring apparatus, his head cocked to the side, his left hand stroking the blue surgical mask covering his chin. The one and only sign that someone in the room was worried was a slight lifting of the head by the assistant surgeon working at the patient's legs.

Without moving his left hand from his chin and without straightening his head, Dr. Warenke gently tapped the monitor screen with the middle finger of his right hand.

Nothing.

The two assisting nurses raised their heads.

Dr. Ballentyne raised his head.

Time pased, a few seconds of it.

And then, still without any movement of his left hand or his tilted head, Dr. Warenke's right arm swung round in a smooth half-circle and the heel of his right hand rapped sharply against the side of the delicate apparatus.

Still nothing.

Another pause.

And another sharp rap with the heel of the hand, followed by an even sharper shot with the closed fist. And, marvel of marvels, the monitors started up again!

All the heads in the room immediately lowered and the tempo of work resumed without any comments being made. Dr. Warenke returned to his post on the high stool next to the head of Mrs. Palmer.

After the operation was over and I was having coffee with Dr. Ballentyne, I told him how impressed I was with the relaxed atmosphere of the procedure, how everyone worked so well together without any fuss even when something was going wrong. In fact, when there was a burgeoning emergency, it seemed to make everyone even more relaxed. "There is something very American about this," I said. "This is exactly what we're good at. We are really and truly at home with machinery. That is the aspect of the human mind that we seem to occupy with most ease."

Dr. Ballentyne agreed with me. "We've been trying to teach this procedure to some visiting doctors from China," he said, shaking his head. "We've been trying for months. You wouldn't believe what a mess they make of it! Just yesterday, they were trying it out on a dog and some little thing went wrong. Something always goes wrong in every operation, I don't care what it is. Well, something went wrong and I'd hate to tell you what it was like. Everyone went completely bananas! Blood everywhere; people running around, sliding and falling down, shouting. Well . . . " he sighed and made a gesture of helplessness.

"It's just not their thing," I said. "I just can't imagine anyone else being as good at this sort of thing as we are. We're not so good at other things that the Chinese people or the Germans or the French do so well. But when it comes to machinery and to fixing things, we are simply the best in the world. That's what we should be doing all over the world—fixing things. Unfortunately, just because we're so good at fixing things, people imagine we're good at feeling what's true or organizing the subtleties of communal life, which is simply not necessarily true."

We shared our impressions of other cultures and their sad attempts to incorporate American technology. Dr. Ballentyne spoke of the feeling he had about this on a recent trip to Thailand. Nothing American actually worked there, he said. On the surface, a little, but right under the surface, the jungle was poised to burst through at any moment and devour all the machinery. I matched his impressions of the Far East with my own experiences in the Middle East, where at one moment I was marvelling at a civilization that could construct the Blue Mosque with a sensitivity and exactitude far surpassing anything Americans had ever done, while a moment later I was shaking my head in disbelief at their inability to do something as simple as hang a bathroom door or make a phone work.

I pressed my point further with Dr. Ballentyne. The genius of American medicine, I said, was brought home to the world in 1981 with the attempted assassination of President Reagan. Who will ever forget the modesty, good humor, and extraordinary skillfulness communicated on the television screen by the physicians overseeing the treatment of the president's wounds? Not the slightest sense of mystification, withholding, or confusion—only a sense of order and organization of information, a relaxed, firm plan of action, a rationale for every possible decision. There were the extraordinary diagrams of the bullet's trajectory inside the president's body—the whole thing entirely like the space mission.

Dr. Ballentyne confirmed my views about the medical handling of the attempted assassination. "There was a remarkable absence of bullshit," he said. "But what the public doesn't realize is that this is going on every day in hospitals all over the country."

"Of course," I said. "Why else do leaders from around the

world come to the United States when they need serious medical care? Our technology and our technicians are extraordinary. American medicine is obviously the best in the world."

Dr. Ballentyne put down his coffee cup and looked at me.

"Then what is your problem?" he said. "Why are you lecturing to us or writing a book, or whatever it is you're doing?"

It was here that I was consciously struck by the difference between the personality of Dr. Ballentyne's face, and the eyes and hands I had seen during the surgery. The face was just a human mask rather than a surgical mask.

"In the first place," I said, looking at his eyes and not so much at the personality of his face, "I write books for the same reason, probably, that you do surgery—because I'm looking for life and service to something true.

"But in the second place," I went on, "I know and you know that medicine is more than good technology. The name of the game is care. I know and you know that. A price has been paid for this good technology, a high price. In the whole of our lives, not just in medicine. But what is care? That's what I want to explore in my seminars at the hospital. What is care? And why is it the most important thing in medicine and, I should say, in life itself? Do you follow me?"

"Not really," he said. Dr. Ballentyne was tired and I was not being clear. I should say, his face was tired. His eyes were as bright and alive as they had been in the operating room.

"What you do in surgery is magnificent. People of older times could never have imagined the accomplishment of such technology. It's wizardry!

"But what you don't understand, what we don't understand, is that in other cultures and in other times there were even more extraordinary accomplishments in the realm of human relationship, what is weakly and hesitantly referred to nowadays as ethics, or even worse, as therapy.

"In my seminars, I am trying to open up this whole question of an entirely astonishing scale of accomplishment in the field of human relationship.

"In ancient times and in other cultures, as I have come to understand it, there sometimes is to be found a power of relationship between one human being and another that is in its way even more awesome than the achievements of our technology. My only complaint against our technology is that it obscures this other human power that is perhaps even more necessary to our lives than advances in the mastery of physical nature. And since it obscures the realities of this other human power, we are prevented from seeing that as the years go by we are gradually losing our possibilities in this realm of human relationship. And without developing these possibilities, we will be defeated by nature far more surely than if we fail to develop our physical technologies."

Dr. Ballentyne began to get interested and I saw that I had found a way of speaking about *care* that connected it to serious ideas about man's place in nature. For me, this discovery was new and immensely promising, as it obviously was for the tired Dr. Ballentyne. Science itself, technology itself, originates—with such people as Dr. Ballentyne and Dr. Bloom (whom I shall soon describe)—in the human love of truth and the human striving to be a serving part of the whole of the great universal order. How strange that the idea of care between human beings should have somewhere along the line become divorced from the idea of knowledge and the natural order.

But it was now becoming clear to me that this need not be the case. That which science could never discover at the end of its telescopes and microscopes could be discovered in the realities of the doctor-patient relationship. I mean to say that the fact of universal consciousness and purpose, which had been taken as a chimera by the serious scientific thinkers of recent times, could be clearly and unambiguously discovered in the study of the power of human relationship in the doctor-patient transaction. Selfless caring and giving was to be studied as the result and expression of a material energy within the physician's own consciousness, an energy that could be activated only in response to real need by another human being. Precisely this energy could never be seen with telescopes or microscopes, yet it was precisely in order to experience this force that science began in the modern era with such spiritually sensitive minds as Newton, Kepler, and especially Leonardo.

But scientific method soon degenerated into a mere technique, an algorithm, a computerlike program, a mechanical procedure. The mechanical, imitative, reflexlike aspects of the mind began to be emphasized in the doing of science. Intellectul intuition was removed or became only a rare event, while one went on with the gray, everyday businesslike procedures of "doing science." Science became bourgeois. Science became very good at being bourgeois, like a man who is very good at organizing his business and making sums of money. Science very soon not only occasionally stumbled upon a great idea and a miraculous conception of the universal, natural order, it eventually found itself in the miracle business, constantly discovering extraordinary aspects of the universe, nature, the human body, constantly having to revise its entire theoretical structures, producing techniques and technologies that in times past would have stood out as the great invention of an entire era, but which now were being churned out practically on a daily basis. Terms like *information explosion* and *technological revolution* can scarcely do justice to the phenomenal successes of our science in recent decades.

But it is all bourgeois, that is to say, ultimately boring and meaningless. Organizational efficiency, which is what the ideal of scientific method had become reduced to, is a very, very poor imitation of the power of impersonal, nonegoistic feeling that is one of the main keys to mankind's opening the doors to the meaning of living and the real knowledge of the universal order. So while we are marvelling, with good reason, at the greatness of modern science and especially the excellence of modern medicine and medical technology, we are receiving less and less in the way of meaning.

This is why I say that it is imperative for medicine to stay within the fold of science, to resist being understood too easily as a humanistic discipline, as a matter of subjective, personal ethics between doctor and patient or as a matter of social ethics, business contract or as any of the other modalities by which the transactions of the human psyche are nowadays routinized. Keep medicine scientific and at the same time keep the inescapable force of the encounter with death and raw human need.

Keep medicine scientific and only then is there hope of bringing back into science the power of conscious feeling or, as it is also called, direct seeing, or, to give it the familiar name: the intuitive sensing of the Real. As far as I can see, for us modern people this power of direct seeing can be cultivated only within the context of human relationships. There can exist in some of us moments of direct seeing, but these moments do not last and do not influence the whole conduct of life. Through the powers that can arise within human relationship, this kind of direct seeing can be cultivated and can enter more and more into the everyday decisions of life.

The doctor–patient relationship remains one of the last remaining nontrivial forms of relationship possible for modern people. It must be kept within the fold of science because it is science, above all, that needs nourishing by the realities of conscious human energy. That is what I am trying to argue all the time. Don't let medicine become a humanistic discipline; don't let it become technology; don't let it become business. Keep all the science and with it keep the direct encounter between a human being in real need and another human being who is obliged to help him through knowledge of nature and attention to the human self in front of him.

It is science that needs this nourishing of the powers possible for man through human relationship. We are going to be living with and within science for many generations to come. To nourish science must be a serious priority for our culture. This means to see very clearly with which aspect of the mind we actually do our science now, with which mind we actually perform our bourgeois miracles and everyday breakthroughs, such as travelling into space and handling the human heart, so that we will not expect these miracles to help us in any way whatever in our relationship with others, which requires of us quite another aspect of the mind than that with which we now do our science. I am arguing against attempting to make the relationship to the patient routine, mechanical—this is really why I struggle against the whole of so-called medical ethics.

Please understand me. I believe the whole of nature operates on principles of conscious energy. I believe that nature is at least as purposive and suffused with Mind as we, her creatures, are. I also believe there is a strictly mechanical side to nature and even a strictly automatic side. We have become good at knowing the automatisms of nature. That is our genius. This we accomplish by means, largely, of the automatisms of our mind. That is good. It is needed. What science would be practical without this? But this kind of science leads us neither to knowing nature as it really is in itself nor to developing in our own minds the higher and freer powers of choice and perception that alone will enable us not only to survive as a species but individually to fulfill our lives and to fulfill the purposes for which we in fact exist on this earth.

Of course, there must be rules and forms of behavior within which such an important exchange as the doctor-patient relationship takes place. But these forms of conduct must reflect the larger meaning of the exchange and indeed the larger meaning of life itself and conscience itself. The forms of mutual human relationship are not just invented for convenience or for "rational" efficiency.

Yes, I suppose I am going far afield here. The customs and manners by which mankind transacts its mutual relations are one of the forms by which great knowledge has been handed down over the ages. It is not for nothing that the great lawgivers are almost without exception understood as divinely inspired or legendary beings—Moses, Manu, Mohammad.

I must really stop and go on with my narrative. But there is so much to say about all this. And so much to do. In any case, I hope it is clear to you why I reacted so strongly against Dr. Patai's long and eloquent speech about the patient's rights and the doctor-patient contract.

I want to see you. I will tell you what I can in writing, but I need to see you. It's no longer something I just dream about. I need your help in all this. I often travel to the East Coast and could easily come down to see you. Just tell me when.

13. What Is the Work of Man?

This title was not, of course, on anything I handed out to the audience, nor was it ever mentioned explicitly during the meeting. Yet the question of the nature of man's work was fundamental to the whole discussion of the problem of care. And *is* fundamental.

Everyone understands this question of work. It's an ancient, perennial question, and how we deal with it is of enormous consequence in our lives, both as individuals and as a species. From Plato to Marx to the latest psychological theories, the definition and meaning of work is one of the fundamental questions of human life. Just as Freud directed us to the sex question, so Marx directed us to the work question.

I saw Dr. Patai's view of the doctor-patient relationship in this very broad context. What he was proposing was rational, ethical, and justified by all the ordinary, sensible standards of our time. To make the doctor-patient relationship into a contract modeled after the goods-for-services agreements of our civilization made a great deal of sense. No doubt the picture I had of the role of the physician, the role of a man with developed powers of conscience, attention, and intelligence, a carrier of deep—not merely socially acquired—personal authority and force, no doubt this picture was now outdated. As Lewis Thomas has written, this picture was adequate enough when medicine really had no power to do anything. But now that through advanced technology medicine actually can do so much, the image of the physician of necessity is changing and becoming more humanly realistic.

But to hell with realistic! I'm speaking of the world of man's inner being. In which case "realistic" is only another word for "the world of appearances," the world where perceptual illusions and ordinary, egoistic emotions—the comfortable emotions and the familiar streaks of paranoia called love and passion—rule as gods.

At the same time, who am I to argue that people try to face their world in search of something higher than the ego? I am not suggesting that I could fare any better in front of the mess that the modern doctor confronts every day. I can hardly imagine what it does to you to have to face life and death matters in an environment where reality has systematically been ruled out. The paperwork, the committees, the financial planning, the corporate reports, the hospital politics, the proliferation of research literature and journal articles, the tangle of legal considerations, tax considerations, billing considerations, not to mention the wife and the kids, and possibly the wife's psychiatrist and the childrens' personal problems. But leaving aside all the latter, the personal problems that everyone faces nowadays, and limiting ourselves to considering the actual work the doctor actually does—it is a very striking problem: to deal with the really organic needs and events of human life in an environment that is, as it were, increasingly "inorganic," that is, increasingly mental, verbal and routinely organizational.

Unlike doctors of old, you are less and less mixing in with your hands and muscle, less and less using your senses and your body. For example, a good doctor used to diagnose the patient, sometimes, by smelling him. I remember that you yourself used to do this. Perhaps you still do. But what about your students?

No, don't tell me about the classification of odors as a diagnostic procedure. When I say the doctor smelled the disease, I am not saying merely that he detected a specific odor characteristic of this or that disease. I am saying he smelled the patient. But I think you know what I mean so I won't waste more time on this small, but interesting, point.

The main issue is the work of a man and how technology helps and hinders that work, and how to tell the difference. Where has the advance of technology made men weak in their being and in their inner striving? And where has it simply shifted the stage of the real work of man from physical things to mental things? Dr.

Patai's complaints about the practice of medicine—were they not really an expression of the new material with which the work of man is now concerned? Instead of physical things, we must now work with mental things, emotional things. But it is the same work, is it not? The problem is that we don't know how to treat our thoughts and emotions as external things. This is the secret of the work of man in our time. It sounds very simple, too simple. But it is the main question of the day-to-day life of man in our present world. It sounds simple, but although it is simply stated, it is very difficult to put this simple truth into practice.

But I am getting just a little ahead of myself. Before Dr. Patai had his opportunity to elaborate on the difficulties of the present-day practice of medicine, Dr. Gilbert Bloom, the nephrologist, gave his intelligent presentation on the subject of technology, a subject that I introduced in the following way:

"Do we have technology or does technology have us? I would like to try to set this question within a broad cultural context because here, too, something that is happening in medicine may be taken as an illustration of what is happening to all of us in our society.

"The whole of our culture is having a reaction against a long-standing faith in the goodness of science and scientific technology, a kind of waking up, a realization that science has not lived up to what it promised. Throughout the world, people are having second thoughts about scientific technology, even as its influence and our dependency upon it continue to grow.

"In part, this is a waking up from the Western world's naive faith in progress and in the power of unaided reason to understand the world and little by little to solve all the major problems of human life on earth, a kind of scientific messianism, a rationalistic messianism that has been part of our culture for the past several hundred years, very unlike the views of how history goes that one finds in other cultures. Our view of history is more or less linear—the line of time continually ascending. Every day in every way things are supposed to be getting more or less better. That used to be the view we all shared, but it came to an abrupt end about twenty years ago. Among the chief causes of this disillusionment, one can cite the proliferation of atomic weapons and the ecological crisis. But when people speak about this, they almost always point also to their disillusionment with medicine.

"At the same time, through the continuing innovations of advancing technology, every aspect of our lives is undergoing radical change. It is impossible even to imagine the degree of change that technology has brought to our lives. Even from a hundred or fifty years ago. It is a different world. And to go backward is simply out of the question. The question is not simply how to live with it. More than that: The question is how to know just what technology is and what is good and what is bad about it, how not to be fooled by it.

"In medicine it seems quite obvious that the main problems of the day are almost entirely the result of our inability to understand the place of advancing technology in the world and life of man: issues involving costs, the allocation of limited resources, unprecedented ethical and moral dilemmas related to life-support technologies, new and tormenting legal pressures. The issue I am asking us to concentrate on here is how technology affects the doctor-patient relationship. It is upon this issue that all the other problems converge."

At that point I handed the microphone to the nephrologist, Dr. Bloom.

Were I a novelist, I would now spend some time on Dr. Bloom's physical appearance, which contrasted so sharply with his easy, informal regular-guy postures and language. A swarthy-skinned, slender man in his mid-forties, his dark eyes burned with intensity, his lips were turned constantly in an expression of sorrow, even when he laughed. He was the only physician I have met (apart from my memories of you) who gave the impression of having his home in another world, a more real world than our own, the world of real suffering. This fact about him gave him authority.

He spoke very simply. "Well," he said, "I've just made a few notes, a few things I'd like to say.

"I think when you talk about technology, it's probably good to have some general definitions. About science, you could say it's the study of what is. And if you look at technology, it could be called the adaptation of the principles of what is. And that really takes in a lot of things. It may mean the instrumentation in the intensive care unit or it may mean just a new way to run a blood sample. All of that is technology and all of that impacts on us in medicine.

"Probably the first technological advancement in medicine was the invention of the stethoscope. As you know, Laennec invented the stethoscope. It was a simple case of seeing a situation and adapting a physical principle to it. He went in to examine a young woman who was in some type of breathing distress at the time and noticed that many of his surgical colleagues—the barbers of that era—when seeing patients like this would put their ears to the chest to listen to what was inside, be it breath sounds or the heart. Laennec, being a physician and not a surgeon, and therefore somewhat more shy, and knowing that sound could be amplified through objects, took a piece of paper or parchment, rolled it up and listened to the sounds of the chest. And this was the principle of the stethoscope. It was probably the first case where technology actually separated the physician from the patient. And was also an example of an age-old difference between physicians and surgeons that is still probably true today.

"Since that time, especially in the last thirty years, there has been an enormous explosion in the advancement of technology that we all have to deal with on a day-to-day basis. What we don't deal with is the impact it's made on us and on our society and on our patients as individuals.

"If you look at technology and if you look at its application to medicine, it falls into several very broad categories. One of them is preventative—obviously—and some of the greatest advances in medicine have been in this area. Nobody can argue that the dollars that were spent in discovering the cause and prevention of poliomyelitis were not well-spent dollars. Many of us can remember what a great plague that was. And if you look back you see there were approximately $40 million spent—*totally*—in the research into that disease, which is now eliminated! This has been true with many of the infectious diseases. And so, technology in the area of prevention, which we really don't give much thought to, certainly has been very effective—no one could dispute that.

"However, when we look at the technology that we deal with more on a day-to-day basis, I think it falls into other categories whose long-run usefulness we're not so sure of. I'm referring to the areas of diagnosis, supportive care, and curative therapy. And, unfortunately, curative therapy, which is what we all would aim for, literally does not exist, after one gets past antibiotics. I mean, many of the things we deal with are curative of the symptomatology of a long-standing disease, but they do little to the underlying process. Much of what we do is to be able to make very exotic diagnoses in situations where we can't do very much, or in supportive care for acute flare-ups of chronic illnesses. You have only to ask what people are dying from today. They die of the same diseases that they have died from for the last fifty years. Mostly in the same numbers, though *maybe* at a slightly later age.

"So, what we're very good at doing now is making diagnoses, getting people over acute episodes, and supporting them through chronic diseases. We may not be improving the quality of their lives at all. And we do all this at an enormous cost. Whether this cost is justified or not really has up to now been a question that society has not confronted—because technology and medicine have been taken at face value as being important and necessary and valuable, without regard to the cost. But now new social pressures are being brought to bear on the cost question.

"It is also important to look at the effect of medical technology on medical education, as well as its effect on the hospital-physician-society relationship. And last of all on the relationship between the individual patient and his doctor.

"In medical education, the student from the first days is introduced to technological and scientific medicine in a way that almost entirely eliminates what we've been calling here the art of medicine. The enormous advances in technology and the need to keep up with them has made it very difficult for people in the process of education to get a feel for the art of medicine.

"Concerning the relationship of the hospital, the doctor, and society, the explosion of technology has caused enormous outlays of money in what some people have called the medical arms race. It's not rare for somebody in the hospital to tell the administrators that they need a certain piece of equipment in order to be as good as the hospital next door. It's not unusual for an administrator to come to a department to tell them that if we get this or that piece of equipment we'll get more patients. However, it's highly unusual for an administrator or doctor to look at that equipment after a year has passed to find out if it ever did anybody any good, except to increase the billing. And with this in mind, advances will continue to be made and machines will continue to be bought. And this may not be bad, provided they do serve a useful purpose. Technology up to now has not been questioned. It's only been accepted. And that's been the problem.

"And in the patient-doctor relationship, I think that first of all people nowadays like to say that technology has removed the physician from his patient and removed the interaction of the old doctor-patient relationship. I was surprised, when I was preparing for this seminar, to come across a textbook that was written in France in the year 1600 by what would now be called the dean of a medical school. The titles of the chapters were: 'Why Do Physicians Not Spend Time with Their Patients?' 'Why Do Physicians Keep People Alive When They Should Die?' 'Why Do Physicians Make So Much Money?' This is well before transplants and bypass surgery! And so I think many of the negative things about the doctor-patient relationship that are blamed on technology have actually been going on for many, many years. It's only that the technology of today has become more refined.

"In our hospital here, one has only to go into an intensive care unit to see the enormous problems that technology has created with respect to trying to relate to the patient. It brings what's going on into much sharper focus than any other situation.

"A patient develops an acute illness; sometimes it's an older person, sometimes it's a very young person who's never been sick before. The patient is brought into the intensive care unit and immediately all the technology we have is applied to saving the life of the patient or getting him over this acute exacerbation. And what happens at that moment is that the patient loses control of the situation. He may be too sick to do anything in any case, but then it's his family that loses control of the situation. What's happening is beyond their understanding—they cannot grasp the limits and capabilities of what we can do. The patient and the family are usually placed in an impossible situation. The physician is confronted with a very sick person. He knows that he probably has the ability to get him over this acute illness. He never questions, nor can he at that point question, the long-term value of what he's doing, because it's almost impossible to predict in the individual situation. There are studies that tell us that 60 or 70 percent of patients discharged from ICUs are dead within a year. We don't know who that's going to happen to. We can't pick and choose at the time of the acute illness.

"The physician is now placed in the position of trying to apply this technology that usually causes a great deal of suffering and expense to the family and society in order to get the patient through the crisis. The nurses are placed in a position of caring for this patient on a continuing, hourly basis, and they're stuck with the suffering of the situation and often become the 'advocates' of the patient, in the sense of asking the doctor: 'Why are you doing this? We've been through this exercise before—we know they're going to die. Why do you continue to do this?' The physician is then stuck with his decision and usually, not always, it may lead to a very adversarial situation between him on the one side and the nurses, family, and patient on the other side. We've lost the ability to resolve this situation in any way, although some people resolve it by saying, 'Well, do whatever you can all the time and then you never have any problems in deciding if you should have gone on.' The problem with that is that now society is putting limitations on what we can do and technology may have to be placed in quite a different perspective. And I believe this is going to lead to *enormous* problems because of the way we practice ICU medicine.

"On the other side of the coin is the doctor who sits in his office, where all this technology doesn't mean very much because 90 percent of the people who come to see him don't need it. And yet he has been trained to master this technology and to use it to make diagnoses and to give answers. The patient does not come for those technological answers. He comes for some kind of a relationship, whether teacher-student, parent-child, friendship, whatever it may be. But doctors trained today have missed that. So the patient comes to him, the doctor orders a set of laboratory tests and says to the patient, 'Well, you're fine,' and the patient knew he was fine, but he wanted to talk about something.

"In that sense, most of the people that we deal with, except in these very acute situations, don't really need the technology, and we tend to lose sight of that. They don't *need* a CAT scan, they need somebody to hold their hand.

"Now, I believe that the technology is necessary and that it will and should continue to go on. But I believe right now that the technologies that we have are very unsatisfactory. We're not curing the problems, we're diagnosing them, we're supporting people, and we're overselling what we can do, raising the expectations to the public and therefore leading to great disappointment. We sit around and marvel at all the great things we can do, and the family says, 'But he died!' And we say, 'Yeah, but he died in electrolyte balance and three months later than he would have died four years ago.' And that really doesn't make any difference in the long run."

Even more than I had anticipated, Dr. Bloom's talk said every essential thing about technology and the work of the physician as a human being caring for other human beings. It explained why the emotional life of the physician has been less and less nourished by his work and why therefore he is less and less able to care for his patient at the level of intensity appropriate to the level at which the patient feels his own need, or at which the family feels its own need.

And this in turn prevents the energy of feeling from entering into his scientific thought, which consequently sinks to the level of bourgeois automatism characteristic of the practice of science in our contemporary world.

How Dr. Bloom himself reached this degree of sensitivity and impartiality toward technology is another question. I am certain it had to do with a combination of his own natural common sense about the human condition, his repeated experience of seeing the suffering of his patients, and his own personal suffering of which I know nothing. May all physicians aspire to be like him in these essential respects! But the problem is that he himself doesn't know how he came to his understanding and therefore he cannot pass it on to others.

In any case, when Dr. Bloom finished speaking, the relationship between the question of caring for the patient and the development of medical technology was clear, as I had hoped it would be. What was clear was that with all the technology in the world, medicine remained almost entirely a matter of human relationships. With all the science in the world, the actual treatment of illness remained a matter of human relationship, without which the science was not only powerless but even destructive. To sacrifice the right quality of human relationship was actually to sacrifice the quality of science itself! The work of a doctor was the work of human relationship together with the challenge of right action and clear, impartial thinking. And all of this was impossible without the mastery of one's own emotions—in other words, the growth of inner being that is and always has been the true context of what nowadays bears the tedious name of *ethics*.

So the stage was set for Dr. Patai to speak about and to incarnate for every one of us to see the awesome difficulties of separating oneself from one's emotions and thoughts, which is a precondition for the scientific mind and the ethical heart, and which is the key to the real work of man, particularly a physician, in the present era and in the decades to come.

"We will now hear from Dr. Arthur Patai," I said and handed the microphone to him. I noticed how soft his eyes were.

Instead of sitting at the seminar table with the microphone in front of him, he stood up and took a place behind the podium, holding the mike in his hands. After the customary self-deprecating remarks concerning his inability to say anything important on the subject, he began, "Dr. Needleman has asked us to consider the subject of caring. Can we care for the patients? How can we care for the patients? Well, surely it depends on what you mean by care. My views on this topic have changed a good deal over the years in ways that I would never have anticipated on the basis of my early training with such mentors as Dr. Benjamin Kaufman at Hahnemann Hospital in Philadelphia. . . . "

I nearly jumped out of my skin when I heard your name! Dr. Patai continued, "Yes, we can care about the patients, and yes, I do care about the patients—but not in the way I had anticipated I would. It is simply not possible for me to care about my patients in the same way I care about my friends and family. This may seem to you a very obvious statement, but it has taken me years to accept this and I think there are many others in the health-care profession who have not yet accepted it. It simply is *not* possible to care for our patients in the way many of us imagine we should.

"It seems to me that people in the health-care profession have been laboring under the burden of believing that if we were decent human beings, we would care for our patients in a way that is, sad to say, simply beyond our ability.

"Frankly, I demand a certain reciprocity from my patients. I try to be compassionate and understanding with my patients, but I'm aware that I cannot be equally compassionate and understanding with all my patients. I just haven't got enough in me. I feel as though I don't devote enough of those qualities even to my friends and relatives, and I don't know how much I have for my patients.

"I try giving the most compassion and care to those who I think need it most. That's a subjective decision and it usually has to do with age—particularly kids, sometimes much older people, and people who are very, very sick. With others, frankly, I'm a little more sparing with my compassion. And I find, increasingly, that I demand reciprocity. That is, I see patient after patient who wants to be treated as a human being, as a unique individual. And yet, they have very little sense that I too am a unique individual. They see me as a doctor. They bring fear and anger . . . and you know, it's pretty awkward trying to treat somebody with compassion and understanding and care when all they bring you is fear and anger. I think it takes a special person to be able continually to be compassionate in the face of that kind of emotional presence. I feel I'm at my best when I *can* bring these qualities to the patient, but I don't demand it of myself all the time and I think it's unrealistic for any physician even to try to do that.

"Dr. Needleman asks in the handout: 'Is it possible, in the contemporary milieu, for the practice of medicine to be instrinsically rewarding?' And the answer is: Yes, I'm a practicing doc and I like my work. There are some things about it that I don't like, but mostly I like it. I like the sense of mastery I have in terms of skills and understanding and being able to confront the problems that I do in the course of a day. I like, ironically, the *structure* of my work. Just as this podium protects me from you, the audience, where I might feel a little bit anxious, so the structure of the health-care setting protects me. I like that. Because, even though the patient has to be protected from me and people like me, *I* need protection from patients!

"You know, there have been some very good studies recently about how many health-care professionals are *frightened* of patients!

"But one of the things, and I want to stress this, that I enjoy the most, aside from the collegial context of working with others like myself who are trying to be helpful to patients, is being with human beings coping with stress. It's amazing to me that most people struggling with accidents and illness—with terrible problems—they behave magnificently. They bear up so much better than any of us might in the face of pain and suffering. And I find that when I enjoy my work the most it's at the times when I can

ally myself with that coping and assist the patients, and learn
from them. And, ironically, even though I talk about structure
and protection, I find it very statisfying when the patient can see
me as a human being too—limited, fallible, but doing my damndest
to be helpful. And, if there's a sense of the two of us working
together at a joint enterprise, that's deeply satisfying for me . . . "

Dr. Patai was clearly becoming a bit emotional at this point.
He stepped back from the podium and made a collegial joke with
Dr. Bloom. He then went on, after clearing his throat and taking
a drink of water.

"Dr. Needleman asks if medicine is intrinsically rewarding. In
our preparatory meeting he asked me if perhaps caring in the
medical sense has ceased to be rewarding as a work in its own
right and whether therefore docs are insisting on being liked by
their patients as a way of filling the vacuum. Have I got that
right, Dr. Needleman?" Dr. Patai looked at me in the histrionic
way speakers on a panel in front of an audience always look at
each other and have no doubt done so since the time of Ham-
murabi. I nodded back in the same courtly way.

"It's an interesting question," he said with an unconvincing air
of objectivity (this was a very emotional man, whom I could not
help but like more and more as he spoke, even though I saw that
the audience was liking him less and less). "If you ask younger
doctors and students what's most important to them during the
day, it turns out that being liked and respected by the patient is
enormously important to them. Strange, but true, as people age
professionally, that becomes a little less important. Liking the
patient as an individual is less important and having the patient
like you as a doc is less important. What takes the place of this is
your care for your art. You have a sense of what's right and
what's appropriate, and you begin to get a sense that even if you
don't like this person, this drunk who's writhing and throwing
up and calling you names, you're still going to care for that
person as best you can. I might avoid doing some little things
that I might do with a person I cared for more, but I'm still
going to try to do my best by that person.

"But there's another step here. In times not too past, caring was shown in ways that we nowadays categorize as paternalistic—you show your caring by making decisions for the patients that they cannot possibly make for themselves. And it's generally thought that this is now being replaced by, or ought to be replaced by, a system whereby the patient has to make all the decisions himself. That can be done, as I think it should be done, in a caring fashion, or it can be done sadistically.

"But in fact something else is happening that is taking the place of all these alternatives and that is one of the countless factors that altogether add up to making the practice of medicine less and less tolerable for a humane and sensitive human being who wishes to serve his fellow man.

"Dr. Needleman does not like my idea of the contractual doctor-patient relationship. He has a dream of the great physician who is not only scientifically expert, but a wiser and better being than the rest of us. I, too, had such a dream until I realized not how foolish it was, but how impossible of actualization in our present world. And if Dr. Needleman would look at what is happening to us doctors, he would not only drop all his opposition to the contractual idea, but he would embrace it as a blessing in the face of the new alternative that is creeping in among us.

"Paternalism is defined as making a decision for someone else, allegedly for that person's own good. But now, more and more doctors are doing things for patients and the fact is that *nobody* is making these decisions. Just one example: Today, discussing emergency room procedures we were talking about when and where to resuscitate patients who are brought in presumably dead on arrival. Well, for all intents and purposes no doctor in an emergency room makes that decision any more. The American Heart Association standards are that you resuscitate everyone, *everyone*! Unless you have compelling evidence that it's absolutely impossible. So I would say that at least in part, paternalism has been replaced by what I would call "instrumentalism"—that is, the physician has become an instrument of *policy* that has been set in concrete some place far distant from either the doctor or the patient.

"In such circumstances, it's hard to say exactly how you show your caring. Sometimes, it's by ignoring the policy arrived at in a distant way; sometimes you try to implement the policy in as human a way as possible . . . as caring, as, as individualized a way . . . as . . . what am I trying to say?" Dr. Patai stepped out from behind the podium and took a long drink of water. I saw that his shirt was damp from perspiration. The audience was now clearly irritated by him and this also began to interest me. I began to suspect what the whole secret was of the problem of caring. The secret of the problem of the work of a physician. If I may say so: the secret of the problem of the work of a man—in our time and place.

I saw, listening to Dr. Patai, especially following Dr. Bloom, something about the problem of the human emotions that had never been stated in all the literature of religion and philosophy with which I had been acquainted.

I was familiar enough with the idea that man has qualitatively different qualities of feeling and I had even written a whole book about the difference between real feeling and egoistic emotion. Looking at the situation of physicians and most modern people, I had come to the conclusion that the problem of caring for one's neighbor was that one didn't have or know how to cultivate the authentic feelings. This, too, was why the practice of medicine or any other work was ultimately unsatisfying. Meaning in life comes about only through the awakening of one's own real mind, including as a major component one's own real feelings. As I say, I had naturally assumed that the lack of such feeling was the chief problem of the physician.

But after Dr. Patai spoke, I saw that I had been wrong, or rather, imprecise on this score. What I saw as the secret of the problem of caring—I have to confess—struck me as of such immense importance that, although the fact which I saw was sorrowful enough and the way to correct it difficult enough, if not impossible for most doctors, a tremendous wave of joy and hope surged through me.

And now I face the problem of communicating to you not only this discovery, which you may very well consider of trifling significance, but even if you should see that it is important, you are very likely to resist my claim that it is something exceedingly difficult to put into practice.

I shall put it as simply and baldly as possible: Dr. Patai, whom I now take to represent a large number of decent and well-meaning physicians, just this Dr. Patai, your own pupil of recent years, has indeed most of the authentic feelings necessary for the compassionate care of his fellow man and perhaps even for the beginning of an intuitive knowledge of disease. He surely has authentic feelings. His presentation made that abundantly clear. However, in addition to these authentic feelings, he has swarms of inauthentic, egoistic emotions, such as we all have: self-pity, laziness, vanity, habitual and all-pervasive self-justification and imaginary fears of every kind.

What defeats Dr. Patai, and all of us, is the inflexible assumption that one has to destroy the egoistic emotions. This leads to further guilt and self-deception and a form of ontological psychopathology, the likes of which not even Freud was able to imagine.

The point is that man's name is legion. And it is through caring for this aspect of one's being that care for my neighbor is born.

This means treating my own emotions as though they were external beings, giving them one's compassionate but impartial attention. And for this it is necessary to be a physician toward oneself.

Until a man can be a physician toward himself, he cannot be a physician toward another.

Until a man can regard all his own many "I's" as his, so to say, "patients," he can never be free to love another human being effectively, cleanly, with power and intelligence.

Now, doctor, do you understand why I am so drawn to the subject of medicine? As a metaphor of the human condition, of my human condition, it is unparalleled. The whole problem as well as the way out of the crisis of our lives can be seen in a proper study of the role of the physician in the modern world.

I do not seek a "contractual relationship" toward the many

selves that inhabit me. Nor do I seek "paternalistic" relationship to them. I need to study them, study my emotions and thoughts and countless physical impulses—all of which presume the role of "I" when they appear—that take all my energy, until there can appear in myself that freedom of thought and attention and care that is externally represented throughout all times and cultures in the role of the true physician. In calling to you, I am calling to the physician in myself!

14. The Financial Disease of Modern Medicine

This will be my last letter of this kind. I've accepted a speaking engagement in Philadelphia next month in order to come to see you.

More than once I've reached for the telephone to call you and arrange the meeting. I couldn't do it. I couldn't bear just to speak to you on the telephone after all these years—especially as there have been no letters from you since your first replies months ago. I've tried to resist imagining what your silence means or what your opinion has been of all the things I've written. I'll know the answer the moment I see you again in the flesh.

If I haven't yet made clear to you why I need your help in what I am trying, perhaps it will be apparent in this account of the concluding session of the series.

The subject was money.

STATEMENT OF THE ISSUES

The entire medical profession is trembling before the question of money: questions of cost-effectiveness, cost-competition, utilization and acquisition of costly technology, the solvency of the hospital as a business institution, the individual physician's income, the formation of the medical corporation, *etc.* The aim of this last meeting in the current series on human values in the practice of medicine is to examine the extent to which financial considerations are now beginning to take precedence over the welfare of the patient—both in the individual practice of medicine and on the collective level. From where will come the energy to reverse this trend?

You may think it odd, especially in view of how my last letter ended, that I reserved the subject of money for the culminating session. Do I mean to suggest that somehow in the study of money there lies the answer to the problem of the emotions?

That is exactly what I mean.

By way of explanation, I should emphasize something that is probably obvious to you, but is not always obvious to others. The emotions are so much the central question of human life that one is fairly struck dumb by our lack of understanding or even interest in them. For example, if there is such a thing as ethics—whether it be medical ethics or any other kind—then it is a matter of the emotions of man: how to control them, how to evoke the nonegoistic emotions, and how to free ourselves from the emotions that make wreckage of our lives individually and collectively. The question of human relationship is synonymous with the question of human emotions, obviously.

But all our attempts to study and understand the emotions have more or less come to grief. Nowhere are we helped to externalize our own emotions for the purpose of, first, studying them with total dispassion; and, second, freeing ourselves from the destructive emotions in order, third, to create and support in ourselves the nonegoistic emotions for the purpose of which, in my view, human beings were actually created.

To make our own emotions the subject of scientific study has become impossible in the areas where one would be most inclined to seek such a study—namely, in the areas of sexuality, religion, family relationships, and so on. There are two reasons for this impossibility—one of them peculiar to our era and the other common to human beings in all eras and cultures.

Let me very briefly cite the latter reason first, which is that human society has always had the tendency to give high value to identification or submersion in emotion, a condition in which the self-aware energy which properly deserves the name consciousness is dissipated in a functional reaction proceeding in the organism. I refer you to the old James-Lange theory of the emotions for some intelligent theorizing about this state of affairs. Every culture or era has one or two "passions" that it unfortunately places on a pedestal, thereby sanctifying this state of identification with the emotions.

The second reason, peculiar to our era, that the study of emotions has become impossible where one would have been most naturally inclined to find them, has to do with the all-pervasiveness of psychology. Briefly put, modern psychology is the study of other people's emotions. On this basis, no knowledge of the emotions is possible—and this because the attention necessary for the scientifically exact observation of emotion is contained in the emotion itself. In order to see an emotion, the cognitive attention contained in it—an attention that is ordinarily dissipated through fusion with unconscious instinctual responses and associative images—must be liberated through an instantaneous, volitional contact with the attention of thought and bodily sensation.

To put it simply: One can only study emotions by studying one's own emotions—and only at the precise moment one is experiencing them.

And there is no one—practically speaking—absolutely no one who can study his emotions at the precise moment they are taking place, without having mastered the understanding and methods of inner work that come from the ancient and primordial sciences of the self. No psychologist or psychiatrist that you know, no matter how brilliant he is, can study his emotion at the moment it is transacting in him.

No, modern psychology has fostered thinking *about* the emotions, forming theories about them and—in the realm of individual efforts to know one's own emotions—it has fostered the practice of encouraging secondary emotions—that is, emotional reactions to the emotions themselves.

And since psychology has in our time advanced into and fully occupied the spheres of family life, sexuality, vocation and education, it is almost impossible for a practical study of one's own emotions to begin in these areas of human life.

For some reason, however, psychology has almost completely ignored contemporary man's singular relationship to money. The money question is thus virgin territory for the most important work an individual can undertake: the search for real self-knowledge.

I do not say the search can limit itself to the study of the money question. Obviously, it cannot. I say only that for many people brought up in the conditions of modern life, the study of one's relationship to money is the quickest and most acceptable means of approaching the observation of one's own emotions in the moment they are transacting. In all other areas of human life, psychology has cast its net of words and theories, thereby entangling us in mental constructs such that one imagines one is seeing oneself when one is only talking about oneself, either to someone else or to oneself.

Even death and dying have now been psychologized in this way.

But strange to say—or perhaps it is not so strange—money has hardly been touched by modern psychology. Perhaps this is very much in the order of things. Money enters into absolutely everything in the life of contemporary man. It is quite a unique phenomenon. Never before in recorded history, at least not to my knowledge, has money played such an all-pervasive role in human life as it does in our culture. Yet in a very important sense the real influence of money is invisible and it is no wonder that our psychologists do not know how to see it. Like the subject of sex and death once were, the subject of money is as elusive as its influence is all-pervasive. There is nothing about which there is greater hypocrisy in our time—so much so that this hypocrisy is not even conceived of, much less understood. In this respect, the influence of money is for us what the influence of sex was for our Victorian grandparents.

For example, a woman may tell a man absolutely everything about herself—except how much money she has.

Of course, the comparison with sex must be qualified. The influence of the force of sex in human life reaches down to the organic levels of the self. The influence of money is mainly in the personality, the socially conditioned self. But since we modern people are so alienated from the organic forces of our nature, since we all live mainly in the personality, the parallel with sex has its point. Money is the "sex" of the personality.

In our world, money has the power to make things real—to reveal the reality of a relationship or a desire. When the question of money and payment enters into any situation, then, suddenly, it is out of the realm of fantasy and closer to reality.

Money is the great relativizer and reconciler, a force against the tendency of the ordinary mind to trap itself in stark either/or alternatives. There are very few difficulties in everyday life that are not resolvable by discerning the price in dollars that has to be paid. Money quantifies a situation where one wrongly or hypocritically assumes a matter of principle or qualitative difference is at issue. To many people, this is the evil thing about money—reducing human life to calculation. But, as I see it, this property of money is also its great virtue as an instrument of the reconciliation of opposing forces. Money is a third force in a world of opposing contradictions.

I could go on, because, as you see, I am bursting to examine the role of money as the royal road to contemporary man's soul. I know there are people who believe they are free from the question of money. And that therefore it is not so fundamental. They think it is only a question for certain types of people or for people in specific economic conditions. But I can say that I have never yet met a man or woman who is free in this respect. But I will not bore you with more general discussion now. You will see more clearly what I mean as I go on to tell you about this last seminar. The point is only that the question of money enters deeply into the emotional formation of almost all contemporary men and women when they are very young and that therefore there can be no authentic moral development in a contemporary individual until he has squarely faced, through experience, the question of money. In order to externalize emotions, that is to say, to study one's own emotions and thereby seek some measure of inner freedom, without which access to higher feelings like love and the instinctive sensing of reality is impossible, the self-experimental inquiry into money is an absolute necessity for a contemporary man or woman.

Perhaps it is now clear why I chose this question as the topic for the last and culminating seminar. More and more, all over the world, responsible questions about money, such as how much does one actually need, are disappearing from view. Simply to get more money is becoming a force, which very few people even put into question, far less deny in any grown-up way. The original function of money—an extraordinarily creative device sourced in the spiritual understanding of very ancient cultures— has been forgotten.

The physician, even today, still finds himself under an obligation imposed upon him by nature and simultaneously lives in the midst of the passions of the social order. Being absorbed more and more in the world of business and money making—as are all of us—he is still, unlike the rest of us, faced with conditions in which the metaphysical demand upon him to love and care for his neighbor is inescapable.

It is—or could be—an extraordinarily creative situation!

The physician is between two worlds in a way that the rest of us are not. It is given to him as in the nature of his vocation. The rest of us, more and more, must strive with difficulty to discern these two worlds in our lives and inner selves. But, in an obvious way, these two worlds are given to the physician. The world of business, the world of the outer movement of social passion, is confronted by the world in which the laws of compassion are unbreakable. And it is the confrontation of these two worlds or forces that creates the inner conditions necessary for the moral and spiritual development of man.

Is it any wonder that the religious authorities of the ancient traditions insisted that coins be made of a substance such as gold, representing intrinsic value? And that in many cases the ancient coins were covered with spiritual symbols? And is this not the meaning of Christ's dictum: "Render unto Caesar the things that are Caesar's and to God the things that are God's." It is man— standing between Caesar and God, and partaking of both at the same time—who must give the proper attention to each of these two worlds in which he is destined to live. Christ did not say, "abandon Caesar," but rather gave the much more exacting and interesting command to give to each precisely what each requires.

The problem here is that the practice of the art of medicine has now developed into what is called "the delivery of health-care." Health-care is a commodity and falls under, as it were, the laws of "Caesar." Caring for the sick is not and cannot be entirely a commodity for it requires of man faculties that are aspects of the movement toward inner consciousness, a movement that obeys other laws than the laws of rationalistic, societal order. It requires a nonegoistic attention and a nonegoistic intellect. The practice of medicine, therefore, places the physician between the two worlds, and it does so far more obviously and inescapably than any other profession in our culture.

That is why medicine is a sacred art and always has been. It is quite wrong, in my view, to dream sentimental dreams of bringing back some nonexistent and never-existent altruistic physician of the past. No, as I see it, the physician has always been the man between two worlds. Caring for the physical body while attending to the inner man! And his life has probably always reflected this situation of his. He has always had in front of him the question of money, or its metaphysical equivalent, more poignantly than most other members of the culture.

That is why I call medicine "the first science." The physician is the representative of "in-betweenness" in the life of man. As a symbol, he is master of both the mechanical and the conscious side of life. The Great Physician is nothing other than the symbol of the *sage*, the blending of pragmatic action in the external world and conscious devotion to the Higher.

In contemporary terms, the physician is the man who makes money while experiencing the metaphysical facts of life and death in his neighbor. His inner life is, or ought to be, a struggle between the currents of reality that underlie these two halves of his calling: business and inwardness; money and the search for consciousness; paid-for services and spiritual love.

These two currents utterly contradict each other, but only at one level of human life. The physician needs to live this contradiction in full awareness long before there can be any hope of resolving it.

Physician, make thy money! Physician, love thy neighbor!

The question of the financial disease of modern medicine is therefore not the question of making doctors into either saints or tycoons. Nor is it the question of doing away with the financial-rational structure of the corporate world that inevitably is absorbing all of modern life. The power of mind that can find the heart of medicine within that world, that can see the mortal human being, shadowed as he is by an immortal seed of being, needs to be found in the midst of forces that operate in that world. It is the same work that has always called the physician and has always called every serious man or woman who seeks to live a real life of service to the higher. And the key to finding a real life in the midst of the artificial life of society lies in the study of the impulses and attitudes that move man, that move man now and in the ancient past and in any possible future in which life will have a place.

And the principal thing that moves us are the emotions.

Now let me tell you what people said about the subject of money and you will see where the real challenge of this subject lies: how to discriminate between the feelings that move man toward the unity of inner Being and the emotions that motivate the outer life of man? The challenge is to rediscover in theory and then to experience in fact this distinction, the distinction between what in ancient times was called the spirit and the flesh.

The challenge is that the physician no longer has his nose rubbed in physical experience of his neighbor's death—the confrontation with death being the only thing left in our culture that can call forth feelings of the real question of the meaning of human life.

15. The Financial Disease of Modern Medicine (II)

More than in any other of the seminars, I knew what I wanted in this one. I felt very optimistic about it because I felt that in this case I was intentionally on the side of the "devil," that is, the automatisms in man—the fears and cravings—that are associated with money. And I knew that the devil never lets you down. He is always the devil. That is, I wanted the whole evening to get carried away into considerations of political, logistical, and economic issues.

Life, the whole of life, is so suprising! What I soon saw was that, in fact, I had been unconsciously on the side of the "devil" all the time, in all the previous seminars! And that only in this one, where I intentionally sought to study the forces of emotional attachment, where I intentionally planned to allow these forces to show themselves in the fearful, narrow, cunning turns of mind that inevitably gather around the question of money—only now did something of distinctly new and better quality emerge in the discussion!

In short, I saw that all this time I had been too "heavy," too eager to bring in "great" ideas. But simply by attentively watching the forces play themselves out, what I had been seeking all along began to peek through the surface.

My first speaker was an old friend, a very serious woman whose occupation in life was in public relations for Blue Cross of California. We had agreed in advance that she would present a straightforward explanation of the new "Preferred Provider Insurance" plan whose purpose was to hold down the costs of medical services by contracting only with those hospitals and physicians who accepted well-defined limits to amounts charged for the treatment of specific illnesses. As you know, this idea has sown panic among doctors not only here in California, but throughout the country.

This presentation by my friend began as nothing more than a pleasant *aperitif*. She proceeded to outline—simply, firmly, and with considerable warmth—the structure of the new insurance plan that so many physicians were sure was going to take income away from them. And for some of them, of course, this indeed is true. For some of them, there was good cause for a certain degree of concern.

Such was the tone of her presentation. She showed how, from the point of view of Blue Cross, the new plan was logical and justified. I couldn't but be struck by the quality of rapt attention in the audience, nor could I help noting to myself that if doctors could give this kind of attention to their art, they would never have had to be giving it to my friend's discourse on the subject of the curtailment of their income.

Of course, it has always been easy to make jokes about doctors and money. But this observation of mine is intended as more than just a joke. There are very few times in my life when I have seen such riveting concern in the faces of an entire audience. And the questions that emerged just after my friend spoke—these questions were absolutely honest, real, gut-level questions! Someone might say they were all motivated by fear, greed, or whatever, and that is also true, very true. But along with these questions, there also appeared other questions, sometimes asked by the same person who a moment before had been speaking about matters relating to his investments, or his cash flow, or his office overhead and multihospital privileges. And this second kind of question and observation was directly and purely about their art and calling, and was infused with the original love of medicine that they—each of them—once felt when they were beginning, or even when they were very young, as I was when I first met you.

Why this strange development? Why did something pure and real finally appear in these seminars only on the occasion of that subject that for many, is the most seductive of all—money?

The answer, as I see it, is that on this occasion, around this subject, a real separation of the two sides of their nature was able to take place. The threat to personal income on the one side and the love of the art on the other. Quite simple and yet immensely difficult and rare.

I will tell you something that I saw in several of them. The prospect of taking considerable financial losses, even while it seriously disturbed them, also brought a certain look in their eyes, a certain "coming home" and release. I believe that inwardly in that moment, and in one stroke of resolve, they were recommitting themselves to the art. They would go on—perhaps they pictured themselves treating fewer patients or losing certain privileges or breaking rules in order to give the proper care to their patients. But they would go on. Others were no doubt making mental compromises, figuring their way around the new situation—but not all of them. Of this I am certain.

Can you understand it when I say that this development was for me the climax of the whole series of seminars?

By being taken, drawn, seduced, as it were, by the problem of money, all their pretenses fell away. All hypocrisy and self-moralizing manipulation fell away for a moment. And simultaneously with this movement away from themselves there appeared, all by itself, the return movement toward themselves, toward their inherent love of truth that had for so long been covered over. These two forces existed simultaneously and were, to me, so clear, distinct, and separate in them that I was stunned. I had the sense, which I always have on such occasions, that I had come across an entirely new and fundamental truth about the nature of man. And yet at the same time, I was verifying for myself an ancient and eternal teaching about the two natures of man, a teaching that I have spent the whole of my adult life studying and attempting to put into practice.

I saw, too, that the whole series of seminars, with all the ideas I had so clumsily attempted to introduce, had been necessary as a precondition for this fleeting moment of separation to take place in them.

But now I must try to be quite precise and sincere about this climactic moment. Seeing this moment of real separation in them was *my* reward, not theirs! They, themselves, had no chance to take it all in this way, There was no possibility of their recognizing this moment for what it was, namely, a moment in which real self-presence was possible for them.

I can restate my observation as follows: As the emotions about money flashed through the audience, most of the doctors simply lost themselves in those fears and became frankly mere profiteers in their minds and hearts. A small but significant percentage of the audience, however, experienced both their own egoistic emotions and their authentic, impersonal feeling for the art of medicine. I allow myself to believe that the preceding weeks of hearing about the larger meaning of the art of medicine made it possible for this pure feeling to make itself known once again in them. However, even these few doctors were unprepared for the appearance of the moment of a relatively real separation in themselves between the two natures that make up the given being of every man and woman. Being unprepared for seeing both their egoistic emotions and their inner love of truth, they automatically identified themselves with the latter.

I know from experience that this process of identifying oneself wholly with one's higher impulses leads ultimately to nothing of lasting value either for individuals or for the collectivity. In the end, it only succeeds in covering over the ordinary emotions, whose energy must willy-nilly manifest itself somehow, and often in forms that lead to further conflict and sorrow for all people.

The power and intelligence we need to solve the problems of our life on earth cannot come to us in this way, of this I am certain. Only through the appearance in ourselves of an attention that can care for both sides of our nature can we develop into the transformed being that is the real meaning of the symbol of the Great Physician, or, as it was called in ancient times, the "priest-physician."

The appearance of this holy level of consciousness depends entirely on whether or not there has taken place in the individual a correct separation, along precise structural lines, of the two fundamental energies of man's psychological nature, the outer and the inner movement, the "devil" and the "angel."

And the whole, entire problem of being a physician in the contemporary world lies here—or, rather, again putting all my cards on the table, herein lies the whole entire problem of living a real human life. The point is to find the real lines of division and separation within oneself in a constantly changing external cultural environment. In this new cultural environment, the old, hallowed guidelines for seeking out this proper division have been blurred or distorted. The old language no longer points us to the correct division—I mean the old language of religion and ethics.

In this realm, the ground has shifted, but the maps have stayed the same. The divisions and distinctions of our culture do not correspond to the essential divisions and distinctions within human nature. Our society is perhaps further than ever from being a mirror of the whole of human nature—and to be such a mirror is in part the very meaning and function of society itself. Society is meant to be the whole human being writ large.

I will spare you my theories of society. The point is that the divisions between "good and evil," "whole and part," and so on — the classifications, the castes, the specializations and compartments of a culture need to correspond in some measure, even if only very crudely, to the real divisions and functions within the human self. In our time, they do not at all, not even remotely. And the situation is getting worse.

Nevertheless, the laws of reality remain the same. The two forces remain within every human being, as does the call of the third or reconciling energy, the true Self. The aim of my search, therefore, is to find again and again in myself the real division and then the real reconciliation of the whole of the human being.

But what do we now find in our outer environment?—ever more unreal divisions and misleading maps being invented by the changing culture around us.

It is especially painful to find these unreal and misleading divisions being formed in just the area where the last chance exists for people—honestly and without psychologizing—to come in front of the outward pull of the personal impulses, namely, in the sphere of money. Until now, the physician had a distinct advantage over most other classes of society in that it was given to him—if only in a preliminary fashion—simultaneously to be in front of the two currents within himself: on the one hand the wish to understand nature and help one's mortal fellowman, and on the other hand the desire to make a significant amount of money for oneself.

And so, when the next speaker began, I saw the hopes I had felt begin to fade away like the color in an artificially dyed Oriental carpet. This speaker was none other than the chief financial administrator of the hospital, as gentle and sensible a person as one would ever hope to meet. In his talk, so brief and modest, without the slightest attempt to encroach on any area beyond his expertise, he waved a magic wand that returned to the faces of every doctor in the audience that singular and unmistakable expression, so pervasive in our lives, which in this case might aptly be termed: "the satisfaction of transforming the inner Question into an outer Problem through the application of a label." Or, as it might also be termed: "the substitution of a transitory societal conflict for an eternal, inherently human struggle through the acceptance of metaphysically superficial distinctions." In short, the awakening power of the question of money—the opportunity for physicians to approach the question of the two natures of man— was completely obscured. And it is this obscuring of the inner Question of human life that surely represents the real disease, financial and otherwise, of modern medicine.

The chief financial administrator spoke as follows:

"From my point of view," he said, "the difficulty of our problem stems from two points of view, each of which makes sense when examined in isolation, but which are totally incompatible when examined together. I mean, specifically, on the one side, the *micrologic*, the level of decision making as it pertains to a specific patient and, on the other side, the services that are being administered to that patient. I believe that if you were to bring people from the legislature, or from the bureaucracy, to the bedside and ask them, 'What is it that we are doing with this patient that is wrong?' the physician and the health-care delivery systems would win that argument every time, with very few exceptions.

"However, when you take people inside the health-care delivery system to Sacramento or to Washington and you confront them with the problems that are being administered there, then you are at the level of the *macrologic*. All of a sudden, the health-care policies with all their faults begin to make sense, because when you are trying to solve the problems at that level, in the context of schools, highways, health care, unemployment, and everything else, and when you see the health-care policies from that point of view, you cannot draw the conclusion that there is anything illogical or wrong, sad to say.

"Both of these points of view make sense and that's the dilemma. It would be so much easier if you could clearly point to one of them and identify some basic failure in the reasoning, but my experience is that it isn't there. When I'm with the people in the hospital close to the physicians and the patients and the nurses, then my mind says: 'That's the right answer!' But when I go to Sacramento and listen to the chairman of the Health Policies Committee, then my mind says 'That makes sense!'

"They both make sense and it's incredibly frustrating. And I only hope that one of the things we can derive from tonight's discussion is to open a dialogue between the micro logic and the macro logic. Thank you."

With that, the chief financial administrator stopped. What could I say? I made a futile attempt to suggest, through telling an amusing story, that the whole Problem, as outlined by the chief financial administrator, lay only on one of the sides of the truly fundamental distinction between the two currents of human life. This story is from the Middle East and hints at the idea that problem solving in life itself ultimately leads nowhere without a finer awareness of the mechanical way the ordinary mind divides things. The subject of the story is the "wise fool," Mullah Nasr

Eddin who is asked to judge a dispute between two villagers. The first villager presents his side of the story, after which the Mullah exclaims to him, "You're right!" But after the second villager presents his side of the story, the Mullah also exclaims to him "You're right!" At this point, a bystander intrudes: "Mullah," he says, "what are you doing? They can't both be right!" At which the Mullah exclaims to him, in exactly the same tones, "You're right!"

Everyone laughed heartily at this story, but since it had taken me twenty years to understand it, I really had no illusions that it would retrieve the feelings of those few doctors in the audience who had experienced something more inner in themselves during the first presentation by my friend from Blue Cross, in which they had found themselves for a moment in front of both their emotions about money and their love of the art of medicine.

But I didn't mind. I now knew there was hope—if not tonight, if not with this group of doctors, then later, somewhere else, with another group. I thought of you with special intensity then, while I only half-listened to the next and last speaker, Peter Gardena, a practicing physician. Like Dr. Patai, like the chief financial administrator, like so many of us, he was a decent man, in fact a very decent man. I only half-listened as he ran down the field with the ball thrown by the chief financial administrator. Dr. Gardena drew the distinction between what he called "the identifiable patient" and "the statistical patient." The former was the actual sick human being in the examining room; the latter was the patient as representative of general socio-medical-financial problems and patterns. The doctor, he said, must give his all to the identifiable patient in front of him. But when the doctor steps out of the examining room, only then must he give his energies to the statistical patient, and so on. A first-class presentation it was, and it answered everything . . . except the real question.

In fact, from that point on, I thought of you so intensely that I almost hallucinated that you were there sitting in the front row of chairs. I now understood exactly what I needed from you. I understood exactly why I have been writing to you.

I mean to say: I knew what your colleagues need from you. It is not words, not ideas, not philosophy. All of that is necessary, and perhaps people like me can help to provide it. But what they need from you is something only you can provide.

They need to see what I saw so clearly in you when I was a child, something which I believed all grown-up men and women had.

I refrain from giving it a name. All that I have written you is an attempt to speak about this quality. In fact, all that I have written in my whole career is about this.

But if I do not give it a name, some Dr. Gardena or chief administrator will find a label, so permit me to use the word for it that was chosen by G. I. Gurdjieff and that is perhaps the only word in the English language that still has no associations and is therefore down in the depths equivalent to what the ancient teachers in our half of the world called "fullness" and that in the other half of the world was called "emptiness." The English word is *being*.

I cannot, of course, judge the degree of your being. I only know I saw it in you when I was young. Since then, perhaps you have only acquired knowledge, information, position, family, wealth. It doesn't matter. In fact, it is good. Your colleagues, too, have acquired knowledge, position, family, and wealth. What they need to see in you is how these "goods" of life dispose themselves in a man of being. I, even if I had a measure of real being, have not acquired their "stuffing," as you have. They need to sense that there are two lives in you and that in you these two lives have or can become one life, one real life.

I believe you have become two, doctor. The two-ness that is the reality of human nature in its essential metaphysical structure. In this you are possibly unique among the members of your calling.

But have you also become one? This is what *I* need to know.

I'm on my way to you.

III. TO THE READER: TOWARD A NEW BEGINNING

16. Dr. Kaufman

I arrived in Philadelphia late in the afternoon and went right to my hotel. After a short rest, I tried fitfully to outline the lecture I was scheduled to give the following evening. My plan was to telephone Dr. Kaufman in the morning and visit him on the day after my lecture.

But it was impossible for me to think of anything else but him. So the next day, instead of quietly working on my lecture, I found myself in a rented car driving through the familiar streets of my childhood in the direction of his house.

Why I was driving though these streets I cannot say. I knew that Dr. Kaufman had long ago moved to another part of the city, my old neighborhood having long ago deteriorated into a ghetto.

I parked in front of the house that used to serve also as his medical office and got out. Like every other house on the block, it was in bad disrepair. The paint was peeling, the little front lawn was overgrown with weeds, and the cement steps that led up to the front door were chipped and cracked. What had once been a stately, glass-enclosed front porch was now nothing more than a row of twisted, weather-beaten planks.

I stood in front of the house for some time. I realized I was waiting for something, but I could not say for what. Two small, black children, dressed for school, came out of the front door and down the cement steps. They raced past me as though I were invisible.

Suddenly I noticed the broken stump of a wooden post hidden in the weeds of the steeply sloping lawn. Brushing aside the weeds, I climbed up to the stump and recognized it as the post upon which the doctor's shingle had hung. Old memories began flooding into me. It was these memories I had come for.

With the image of Dr. Kaufman's face now vividly before me, I went back to my car and drove off. But as one of these memories is especially relevant to what was soon to take place, I will relate it here.

I was sixteen years old and it was the beginning of a summer that promised to be full of wonder. I had been invited as one of a handful of high school students throughout the country chosen to spend the summer months working and studying at the Jackson Memorial Laboratory in Bar Harbor, Maine. The Jackson Laboratory was, and still is, one of the leading research centers in the field of genetics and cancer research.

Two weeks before my departure, my family, including my favorite uncle and aunt, ceremoniously presented me with the gift of a heavy, high-powered Bausch and Lomb microscope—the real thing, securely bolted in a sturdy wooden case, with swiveling, tripartite objective lenses at the bottom and a set of four eyepiece lenses to be inserted at the top, depending on the magnification desired. I nearly fainted with joy.

But how to operate this magnificent instrument? No one had the slightest idea, not even my father who had a magic touch with anything requiring manual skill, nor my beloved uncle who seemed to know everything about machines of all kinds. This sophisticated piece of scientific technology was out of our league. The microscopes I had learned to use in my biology classes at high school were like a child's toy compared to this.

After two days of examining simple things like sugar, salt, and insect legs and after countless frustrating attempts to use the highest power in order to examine my own blood, which to my mother's horror I boldly stroked out of my own thumb with a sterilized sewing needle, we all hit on the idea of asking Dr. Kaufman to show me how to use this instrument.

So there I was in his office unbolting the great apparatus and setting it on his laboratory table, next to his own microscope, an even more elaborate piece of equipment than my own. Three things stand out vividly from that hour with him. Once again I drew blood from my own thumb, but this time with a spring-loaded metal lancet and I remember the deftness with which he made a smear of the blood on the glass slide and added the necessary amount of Wright's stain, customary for performing a differential count of the various types of blood cells. But more than that I remember two special smells. The first was that of the balsam oil that was needed in order to attain a specific light refraction between the objective lens and the slide—without this kind of oil it was impossible to see anything, and this neither I nor anyone in my family had known. I loved that smell with my body and emotions: pine trees, sweet air, mountains, every sweet memory of childhood wanderings in the woods.

But the second smell was of an entirely different nature: the smell of the ether needed to clean the slides. It was the same smell I had known so well when I had conducted my young and clumsy experiments with fruit flies in my own makeshift laboratory in the basement of our house. The ether was needed to anesthetize and kill the little creatures. It was the same smell that I had lived with later during a long summer working as a medical laboratory technician when I had to kill at least one female rabbit every day in order to perform the then popular Aschheim-Zondek pregnancy test. I would anesthetize the rabbits with the ether and then inject an air embolus into the ear vein. When the embolus reached the heart, the rabbits would thump around unconsciously and die, a pathetic sacrifice on the altar of human sexual confusion.

I was physically repelled by that smell and it had absolutely no pleasant associations either in my thoughts or in my emotions. Except for one association—namely, the experience of study and experiment. There is vividly impressed in me the recognition, repeated countless times, that something in me wished to study and learn, and that this something in me was entirely separate from the desire for physical pleasure or the desire to relive in my imagination emotionally happy experiences of the past.

Dr. Kaufman rather firmly instructed me in the details of preparing slides and working the various lenses. He also insisted that I stay there until I was able to look through the eyepiece with both eyes open, concentrating my attention so that I could look through one eye even though the other was also taking in surrounding impressions. And all the while, the smell of ether was filling my brain and body with a slight physical nausea and dizziness. Whether or not he knew how I was reacting to the ether, or whether he was acting on his own instinctive sense that there was proceeding in me a special kind of suffering, perhaps one of the few authentically honorable struggles possible for man, namely, the struggle between the wish for truth and the compounded resistance to this wish that expresses itself through the physical body and the acquired personal emotions—whether Dr. Kaufman knew or sensed this, I cannot say. I only know that from that time on the smell of ether—a substance that functions generally to induce sleep—has always had an awakening action on me, reminding me instantaneously that there exists somewhere in myself a desire for knowledge that is independent of the automatic pleasure-seeking impulses of the physical body and my acquired egoism.

Dr. Kaufman's house was at the end of a quiet, tree-lined alley in the fashionable Liberty Hill section of downtown Philadelphia. I could have walked there from my hotel.

I nudged my rented car over the eighteenth-century cobblestones and parked directly in front of the elegant colonial house. Instead of a black shingle hanging on a wooden post, there was a small, burnished copper plaque on the front door that read:

BENJAMIN E. KAUFMAN, M.D.
Internal Medicine

I sat in the car for a long time, just looking at the complicated, dark red brickwork of the front wall. I felt nervous and foolish. It was ten in the morning. Although I had written that I was coming, I was here unannounced and he was probably not even at home.

I rang the bell and no one answered. I rang again and waited. Just as I was about to leave, the door was opened and I found myself looking into the clear blue eyes of a strikingly beautiful woman. I glanced at the plaque again to make sure I had the right house and then, collecting myself a little, I asked if Dr. Kaufman happened to be at home.

"You must be Dr. Needleman," she said softly. "Please come in."

The woman ushered me into a small, oval-shaped drawing room furnished with brass lamps and tufted leather chairs. Several small, antique Oriental carpets were scattered over the intricately inlaid parquet floor.

She sat down across from me and introduced herself as Dr. Kaufman's niece. Her name was Myriam Schira and I learned that she and her husband were themselves doctors, pediatricians. I gathered that she was in her early thirties, but at times she looked very much younger. When the sunlight struck her face, highlighting her pale yellow hair, she seemed hardly more than a child. At other times, especially when speaking about her uncle, her blue eyes darkened, giving her the appearance of a mature and exceedingly purposeful and strong-willed adult.

"We had no idea when you were coming," she said, "but my uncle is eagerly looking forward to seeing you. Are you pressed for time now?" When I said I was not, she offered me coffee, which I accepted, and she disappeared for a moment. She returned with a tray of coffee and biscuits. We began to talk.

I learned that Dr. Kaufman had been in failing health for the past year and that he had gradually been forced to curtail all his activities except a limited private practice, which he now conducted here in his home. At this moment, in fact, he was seeing patients and would not be free to see me for quite some time. I indicated that I would wait as long as necessary.

When I asked about the course of Dr. Kaufman's life, Dr. Schira painted a portrait for me of an exceptionally active career. Dr. Kaufman had run a large medical corporation, had directed the medical education program at two major hospitals in the Philadelphia area, and was a leader on numerous examining boards and agencies. He had also been heavily involved, since the death of his wife ten years ago, with several presidential advisory commissions in Washington. He had travelled extensively and had devoted a great deal of time and energy to helping Third World countries modernize their health-care systems. Dr. Schira was particularly fascinated by this aspect of her uncle's work and described his efforts in Iran, before Khomeini, where he was working in remote villages with the traditonal tribal doctors known as *hakim* or "wise men." He had brought back many fascinating stories of the kind of medical practices that were rooted in the ancient Persian culture.

Dr. Kaufman had no children, but it was clear that Dr. Schira regarded him as though he were her father. Since his illness, she had reduced her own schedule to be with him here and help him in any way she could. I had the distinct impression that there was not much time left to him. This suspicion of mine was soon confirmed.

After we had talked for a while and finished our coffee, Dr. Schira suggested that I wait in her uncle's study. I followed her up the stairway that led from the vestibule to the second floor and into a darkened room. She pulled back the curtains and the room filled with light. Against the window was a heavy, antique oak desk upon which were several neatly stacked piles of papers. I could see that one of these stacks, held down with a crystal paperweight, was the collection of my letters.

She told me that she had to go to her office and would return at lunchtime. She estimated that her uncle would be free to see me in about an hour. With that, she left me alone, closing the door behind her. I sat down on the couch. My heart was pounding, but my thoughts were quiet.

In addition to the desk and the couch, there were two Shaker-style, wooden chairs against the wall, beautiful in their severity. Between them was a small table upon which there stood an antique brass microscope. When I noticed the microscope, the memory of my own first microscope came back to me again, this time with tremendous vividness, and the room suddenly seemed to smell of ether!

A grandfather clock in another room struck the quarter hour

and then, seemingly without any interval, it struck again. Time no longer existed.

I got up to go toward the microscope but instead went over to the desk and bent over the pile of my letters. I started haphazardly skimming through them, but when I saw that Dr. Kaufman had made numerous marginal notations, I grew excited and started again from the beginning. Some of these notations were nothing more than checkmarks or exclamation marks, while others consisted simply of one or two words indicating approval or disapproval. I will not call attention to these now. Of great interest to me, however, were the places where Dr. Kaufman had made substantial comments and self-observations.

As I now write, copies of these letters with Dr. Kaufman's notations, are right before me, having been sent to me shortly after Dr. Kaufman's death a little less than a month ago.

The first notation occurs at the end of my first letter, where I describe my grandfather's death:

"Medical ethics" did not exist. Flew by the seat of my pants. Still do. But I cover my ass now. "Medical ethics" as the art of covering your ass.
Abe [my grandfather] asked me to tell him the truth. No problem. Death is absolutely no problem. Life is the problem.

The next notation occurs in my third letter, where I tried to write about man as a two-natured being—the impersonal love that is an expression of man's higher nature and that arises in the physician when he sees his patients as mortal egos crying for life. Dr. Kaufman circled the phrase *moral wonder*, which I had emphasized in order to characterize my feelings when I saw the kind of attention he gave these, to me, pathetic individuals:

It was already a habit. The poor bastards kept coming like ants. The world was one huge disease. They were diseases that talked. Diseases in the form of people. Who could afford to feel anything?
Knew one, maybe two, things. Punch-drunk half the time. Had to laugh to keep from going crazy. Went crazy anyway. Best years of my life.

Reading these notations, I was at first startled by their tone and by what I felt as the youthfulness of Dr. Kaufman's mind. This impression was soon eclipsed when I came to the notation written alongside my account of Mr. Patterson's death. There I raised the question about the kind of experiences of life and death that medicine can bring, experiences that enter into one's own instinctual mind and that momentarily draw all the parts of oneself together:

Why is it that my own almost certainly impending death has no relation to the sickness and sufferings of my patients? I had expected the awareness of my death to make me a better doctor. But the truth is I am absolutely the same person with them. I see that the deaths of all my patients over the years are nothing at all like my own death. Jerry is asking about what he calls the metaphysical needs of the patient. I am barely beginning to understand my own special needs in that domain. On one side is my own death, and far, far on the other side is my work and all the rest of my life. There are no words to express what takes place in me when I try to face my death. I only know it is completely separate from everything else. When I think of the aneurysm that is developing in my belly, there is not only great fear but a remarkably even and all-pervasive sensation of existence. In the light of this division within myself, I see that Jerry is wrong. There is really nothing unique about the practice of medicine.

This notation startled me. I sensed in it a greater truth than all the ideas I had tried to express in my letters. I mean to say that I sensed in it a truth at another level.

It is not only that the subject of death relativizes everything else in human life. That is true. But I suddenly saw that the question of one's own death can draw a man toward something within himself that has no name and can have no name. Against this movement inward, all talk about the inner being of man, however authentic and inspired, is no more than a rough approximation. The act, the actual movement toward oneself is quite distinct from all words and ideas, no matter how profound they may be. I sensed with indubitible certainty that Dr. Kaufman was writing from this experience.

I went on reading the notations. I could sometimes see in them the effort he was making to lend a sympathetic ear to my thoughts. But it was obvious that my whole way of thinking was not congenial to him. Sometimes his comments even betrayed a rough derisiveness.

For example, in some of the notations he referred to me as "Professor Jerry"—which made me smile. But what he had to say to "Professor Jerry" was not so amusing:

What does Professor Jerry really know about science? Has he ever seen half the children in an African village wiped out by a disease that could have been prevented by a simple vaccination? I'd trade all the spiritual teachings in the history of the earth for those lives.

And shortly after that remark he wrote:

Spare us all your preaching about higher feelings, Professor Jerry. Our mistakes gnaw at us day and night. All we need is to be forgiven. And then, leave us alone! The lawyers on our backs are bad enough. You want to pile on philosophers too?

But then, on the very next page, a marginal notation completely unrelated to the particular subject at hand:

There is nothing sacred about medicine—one dying animal helping other dying animals. Only if a man is man, only then is the practice of medicine sacred, but then so is any other occupation. Either all occupations are sacred or none of them are. It all depends on something in the practitioner—the consciousness of my own death for example, which I simply cannot bring to my work. No, I work to escape consciousness of my death, which has become my second life. This contradiction baffles me. Why did I have to wait this long to discover it?

That was all I had time to read while waiting in Dr. Kaufman's house. Hunched over his desk, absorbed in reading my own letters and his notations, I suddenly felt a strong sensation of presence behind me. I wheeled around to see him standing quite still in the shadows of the doorway. My chest thumped violently and something I can only describe as a sigh of joy escaped from my throat even before I consciously recognized him.

His tall body occupied the whole space of the doorway. He was wearing his white coat and in one hand he held a cup of steaming coffee in front of him. Around his neck hung a stethoscope and a pair of reading glasses suspended from a black band. His right hand rested in the pocket of his coat.

For a moment neither of us moved or spoke, as once again time seemed to stop. Finally, he broke the silence and moved into the room. "Well, Jerry . . . " he said in a voice that simultaneously surprised me and evoked ancient memories. The sunlight from the windows behind me struck his face, which had the same effect on me as his voice: rough, jagged, dry, yet wonderfully strong. Everything I had imagined about his appearance was true, down to the lines and folds of skin around his eyes and lips, but actually seeing him face to face startled me beyond anything I could have anticipated. There was something remarkable about his eyes that I had not remembered. In fact, I had the feeling that I had not remembered him at all, even as the old memories flooded my mind. As he came toward me, I experienced an odd sensation of weightlessness, while at the same time I sensed the pull of gravity down my back and in my lower limbs.

He held out his hand, but I wanted to embrace him. As I did so, he laughed gently and held the cup of coffee out to the side to prevent its spilling. With his free arm, he pulled me toward him and then very quickly stepped back to look at me. That look seemed to last an exceedingly long time and affected my whole body.

I mention these details because, as I soon realized, what was transacting between us at the physical level was far more important than the converstation that took place between us, interesting though that was.

He sat down at his desk chair and motioned me toward the couch. I chose instead one of the wooden, Shaker-style chairs, which I pulled toward him. I wanted to be as close as possible to him. We began to talk—first about each other's course of life. Speaking of my own life, I couldn't help but feel that I was also giving him the history of a sort of disease. Odd, I felt, and even a bit comical. He was still the doctor, no matter what we spoke about.

As we went on talking, finally turning to the subjects in my letters, I began to become more and more interested in the effect he was having on me simply by his physical presence. For a while, it irritated me that I kept slipping into the role of patient, even when we were speaking about abstract ideas, something in which I was the expert. But I soon set aside this irritation at myself and stopped trying to appear different than I was. What was actually happening was so interesting and so full of promise with regard to certain fundamental human questions, that I freely allowed everything just to take its own course. It eventually began to dawn on me, and has now become absolutely clear to me, that all my labored letters and questioning had finally led me toward an answer to the problem I had set myself: namely, the problem of what it means to be a real physician, and even more basically, what it means to be a real man, a real human being.

But I am getting ahead of myself. Dr. Kaufman had picked up the pile of my letters and placed them in his lap. Throughout the conversation he kept flipping through them as we randomly touched on some of the subjects that I had written about. What he liked best, he said, smiling, was the account of my experience dropping the severed leg in the elevator. We both laughed and I did not attempt to point out the reasons I had told that story. Nor did I attempt to correct him when he accused me of belittling the progress of modern science. I did say that I had detected his own second thoughts about the influence of science in one of the letters he had written me. But he now merely brushed that aside.

"There are abuses," he said. "But it's like what Winston Churchill said about democracy, that it seems to be a very poor form of government until you consider the alternatives."

I smiled. "I wonder if Churchill really considered or even knew all the alternatives."

Dr. Kaufman looked at me fondly. "Professor Jerry," he said. He took a sip of coffee, and asked me if I wanted some; I said yes, but instead of going to get it for me, he reached into a drawer, pulled out a styrofoam cup and poured half of his own coffee into it, carefully, without spilling a drop. I eagerly took the styrofoam cup from his outstretched hand.

It was not only that he was older than I, nor that he was my old doctor, nor even that I knew he was mortally ill. I could separate myself from all that. There was something else that I knew had always been part of him, but that now seemed stronger than ever. I could not name it, I could only feel it, sense it. It had a strangely familiar "taste" about it, which I couldn't put my finger on.

And whatever this "something" about him was, it had nothing much to do with his views and opinions about science, medicine, ethics, or anything else. In fact, these views of his, if put down on paper, would have made him sound like a representative of some of the very worst things about modern medicine. There was smugness in what he said about American medicine; there was a good deal of naivete about matters pertaining to "the spirit"; there was much crude misunderstanding about ideas—a kind of primitive positivism and a trust in the scientific establishment; there was an impatience and cynicism in his remarks about recent attempts to bring "humanistic" issues into the training and monitoring of doctors. There was a tremendous lot of of the "old boy" about him. When I mentioned that I had read some of his notations, he simply said he had hoped that I would and let the matter lie, not saying a word about his illness. In short, there was something being exchanged between us that had nothing to do with words or ideas or expressions of feeling. I only know that the longer I sat there, the more alive I became—I mean in the sense of a quiet intensity, a kind of circulation in my body.

As he began to grow tired and the conversation started drawing to a close, my own thoughts began to wander during the gaps in our converstaion. As my mind was thus wandering, I recalled some things that helped me to understand what was happening.

One of these things was apparently not related at all to medicine, but in my idly spinning mind it associated itself with another memory directly connected to the question of what it means to be an authentic physician.

Over the years, my career and my personal interests had brought me into contact with a number of people who were regarded as spiritual leaders or wise men. While a number of these people had not been spiritually impressive to me, others were indeed extraordinary people in many ways. But the occasion that came to mind as I sat there with Dr. Kaufman was a meeting I once had with a Sufi sheik in Teheran. This happened to be a man I was predisposed to dislike. I had heard many bad things about him and had spoken to one or two of his disciples, which only confirmed my antipathy toward this man. These disciples struck me as psychologically sick people—evasive, underhanded, and nervous. At the same time, I had heard reports from reliable sources of very serious harm that this sheik had inflicted on some people who had crossed his path.

One day, the opportunity presented itself for me to meet him. I tried to prepare myself mentally for the meeting. I knew in advance that even if this man were a charlatan, it was going to be quite a different kind of person than all the dubious gurus and spiritual leaders I had met in America. These latter were often people without any real weight at all. I had a strong conviction that the sheik was no California-type guru.

I was brought to the sheik's house by one of his disciples, an American businessman who sweated all the time and acted like a man afflicted. I was ushered into a large, dark room, drably furnished, and the moment I entered the room something began happening in my body. As my eyes adjusted to the darkness, I was startled to see the sheik reclining on a couch at the far end of the room. The American disciple translated the conversation, which was tedious in the extreme. The sheik had very little of real interest to say—he seemed to speak in the most common cliches. But his eyes were like fire, even in the darkness. I began to feel queasy and a little nauseated. I left that room and him as soon as decorum would permit.

But what I took from that meeting was very precious to me— the certainty that people do in fact have emanations of a very distinct and material nature. I had experienced this fact before, but it had always been mixed with mental and emotional reactions of respect and admiration for people who had certain moral qualities that evoked trust in me. The sheik, however, had, for me, only negative personal qualities and therefore in my conscious mind I was dead set against finding anything at all remarkable in him. But I simply could not deny that he had affected my body. Although I left the house hating him, I could not deny that my body was filled with a certain kind of energy that had nothing to do with my mental and emotional reactions.

The other memory that came to mind while the conversation with Dr. Kaufman was drawing to an end was a story told to me by one of the most remarkable men I have known. This individual, whom I knew very intimately and who proved himself countless number of times to be a man of wisdom and veracity, told of his own experience with a serious illness when he was about thirty years old. His condition had commanded the attention of a number of doctors, but it had come to the point that they had more or less given up hope for him. For two weeks, he neither ate nor drank and nothing the doctors could do was helping. Finally, they asked him if he would like to see a particular specialist who would have to be brought in from a great distance. (This was years before the calling in of teams of specialists and consultants had become a standard medical procedure paid for by insurance.) They told him it would be extremely expensive, but that this specialist was everywhere recognized as the top man in his field (what is now called gastroenterology). This is how my friend related the story to me:

"I was very weak, but I remember asking, 'How much?' They said something like $3,000, because it would take a whole day for him to come in order to see me. I agreed to that, and I can still remember this little man coming right into my room without even looking at the charts, which were outside. He came in and *he sat by my bed* and after a little while he just said (and here my friend laughed): 'I think it would be a good idea to give you grapefruit juice.' Then after a little while longer, he left. And from then on, I started getting better. And the fact is that this man was a healer—not a quack or unconventional in any way at all. But he conveyed something to me.

"What is it that a doctor can do to initiate the will to live in somebody? Because obviously, people cure themselves. So what is it that a doctor can do to get started the will to live in somebody who hasn't slept, hasn't taken food or liquids, and is completely exhausted? What is this catalytic function? How do people acquire it? Where do they get it? This is the core of the problem, isn't it? I don't think it's a question of drugs or homeopathy or swinging pendulums or acupuncture or anything of the sort. That's not the heart of the problem at all."

While these two memories were coming together in my thoughts, I saw Dr. Kaufman's head begin to nod. His eyes closed and his head dropped. He was asleep. I grabbed the cup from his hand before it fell to the floor.

I remained in my chair for some time, just looking at him. He now seemed very old, very near death. But the sense of his presence continued to affect my body, quite independently of all my feelings for him and I saw this distinction very clearly. What had brought me to the state of sensitivity in which I was so certain of what was happening I cannot say. But for myself, I had solved the problem of the nature of the art of medicine. Or, rather, and which comes really to the same thing: I had found the real question, the fundamental issue in the practice of medicine. It had to do with something in the physician and in man that is distinctly material and physical, rather than psychological or "spiritual" in the accepted meaning of these terms. At the same time, the materiality of this "something" was not at all known or recognized by modern science.

I thought of all that I'd written about in my letters and realized that all along I had been groping toward understanding what I was now experiencing. Many things began to fall into place for me. But just then I was not able to put it into words. That came a little later.

I saw something else as well. As I sat there looking at the slack, sleeping face of Dr. Kaufman, I felt death in the room. It was not a negative feeling. On the contrary, it seemed to correspond to this sensation of energy in my body and the distinct impression of it as something separate from my thoughts and emotional associations. This sense of death in the room brought everything acutely into the present moment and made everything alive and serious, and intensely quiet. I realized that in all my encounters with Dr. Kaufman, when I was a small boy and later as an adolescent, he was toward me in a way that allowed death to be present, not as something terrifying but as an immensity that put everything in a new order, everything including lollipops and mother, and that allowed in myself an openness to an entirely new quality of self-attention.

Time passed, Dr. Kaufman continued to sleep. There was a soft knocking on the door and I quietly got up to open it. It was Dr. Schira, Dr. Kaufman's niece. Trying not to wake him, I stealthily gathered my coat and briefcase, but before I could leave I heard his voice calling me. I turned around to look at him as he slowly and with some difficulty stood up.

"Before you go," he said, "there's something I want you to have."

My heart went to my throat as I watched him straighten himself and walk over to the antique microscope. He picked it up, dusted the brass casing with the sleeve of his white coat, and came over to give it to me. I took it by the base with both my hands and felt its weight. He looked at me for a long time and then went out of the room toward his office. "I don't have the cover for it," he said, without looking back.

17. Dr. Schira

As I came down the stairs with Dr. Schira, I saw that the dining-room table was set for two people. I did not especially want to stay. I wanted to be by myself. But I could hardly refuse.

Dr. Schira was aware of my mood and the meal proceeded with a minimum of words exchanged. At one point, when I asked her to pass the salt, or something, she requested that I call her "Myriam." That brought me back and I realized that I was with another human being.

She had been wanting to talk to me about my letters, which Dr. Kaufman had showed her as they arrived. They touched her very much, she said, and she had often found herself in the position of defending me to her uncle.

"Sometimes," she said, laughing, "I really did not understand what you were arguing. That was when I defended you most."

"You've just summed up the history of philosophy," I answered.

Then, like a sudden change of weather, she turned serious again. With her remarkable blue eyes opened wide, she said, "I want to find what you are speaking about."

Although the experiences of the past several hours had left me in an unusually open state of mind, I did not at first grasp what she was saying. I automatically assumed she was referring to some aspect of the practice of medicine. And so I started asking her about her own field of specialization, pediatrics.

She perfunctorily replied by describing her work with young children, but then she interrupted herself. She took the glass coffee pot from the heating tray and poured coffee into my cup, and then into her own. "Excuse me" she said, brushing back a strand of blonde hair and looking directly into my eyes, "but you are only here for a short while and I may never see you again. I don't want to waste the chance of finding out if you really have something that I need. I am not a dissatisfied doctor. I am not an impaired physician. My work is very rewarding, as far as it goes. I am not interested in the philosophy of medicine or, really, any kind of philosophy at all."

She blushed a little, but without losing the strength of purpose that had appeared in her face. She offered me a small plate with an assortment of petit fours on it, and continued, "Please excuse me if I seem to be presuming on our slight acquaintance. But having read and reread your letters, I feel I know you well. At times, it seemed to me that your letters were written to me, rather than to my uncle."

I asked her to tell me more about herself. I wanted to observe her and be sure I understood what she was asking. She knew I was taking her very seriously. And, for myself, I knew that here, suddenly *that* had appeared, *that* question. *That* need which is like a miracle because everything else in life seems unrelated to it, everything except death. But which, at the same time, like death, is always present invisibly, the signature of another world that permeates this everyday world of ordinary values, ordinary thoughts, ordinary motivations.

All sense of formality between us disappeared.

I felt she was like a sister to me. And I had had enough experience in my life to know that she needed to feel that in me. Only then could she speak with complete frankness. I could tell by what she then said that in fact she did understand because she spoke about herself with a degree of impartiality that is only possible when one feels that nothing need be hidden.

She did not speak about her past at all, except for a few passing references to growing up amid the social upheaval of the 1960s, the war, the drugs, the disillusionment and anger that all her generation shared. And as for her career in medicine, she said only that she never really believed that anyone had anything essential to teach her; she did not expect to get anything from education except certain necessary information and the legal right to practice medicine.

"I am not disillusioned," she said, "because I never had any illusions about my teachers. I always saw that they were part of a world that had gone sour. I went into pediatrics because of what I felt for children and I have the same reaction whenever I see a child for the first time. How can I put it? They seem to me like a separate species of life. I feel as though God, or whatever created the world, keeps sowing these seeds on the planet and that the whole purpose of the planet is to make these seeds grow. Do you understand what I mean? When I see a child, I see pure sentience. You use words like consciousness and awareness—I grew up with these words, don't forget, and they have strong meanings for me. My whole generation grew up with these words.

"But all that is really not the point. I am not interested in saving the world. I feel that I myself am one of these seeds that has never grown. I dream of things I can't speak about to anyone else, neither to my husband nor even to my uncle. They are both fine men and very good doctors, but what I dream of is incomprehensible to them and I sometimes wonder if what I want is simply madness."

She lowered her eyes. "Do you understand what I'm speaking about?" she said in a voice suddenly soft and fragile. "Your letters reawakened these dreams in me."

We finished our coffee. Each time that I began to say something, my words seemed inadequate and I kept them back. With the whole of my being, I felt the reality of what she was speaking about. But I knew, from long experience, that whenever this need for *something else* appears in a human being, whether it is in oneself or in another, it makes all one's ready-made answers hollow. And of ready-made answers I had plenty.

I knew this whole state of affairs very well, when one is in between the old answers that no longer serve and the new answers that one desperately needs. While I was thinking these thoughts, all of a sudden she raised her eyes to me and said, "Thank you."

I was completely taken aback. At the same time, the sense of bond between us was very strong, very strong.

After a few minutes, I suggested that we move into the living room. I did so and, after making a telephone call to her office, she joined me. The new surroundings made it possible to just talk.

I began by asking her in more detail about Dr. Kaufman's illness. She responded with considerable scientific detachment, displaying her grief only at the end. It was unquestionably an aortic aneurysm. Surgery was extremely risky and even in the best case would probably not prolong his life significantly. He had chosen, instead, to live out the time left in as normal a way as possible, devoting himself to his private patients at home.

"Is there absolutely nothing to be done?" I asked.

"Nothing," she said. Then she collected herself and said, "You knew him long before I did and I know from your letters what he meant to you when you were young. Now that you have seen him again, what is your opinion of him? Has he changed very much?"

As soon as I began speaking to her about my experiences of the past several hours, I realized that my recent impressions of Dr. Kaufman, even though I had not yet fully digested them, were the only basis upon which I would be able to respond to the heartfelt confession she had put before me at the end of our lunch and to which I had been able to respond only by a silence that in part represented my instinctive unwillingness to offer merely mental or emotional replies to a question that came from the inner being. And so I decided to answer her in as much detail as possible and to include in my reply what I now understood, on the basis of seeing Dr. Kaufman, to be the culminating chord of all the ideas I had put in my letters to him. In sum, I found myself speaking to her about several things at once: my impressions of Dr. Kaufman, my newly focused views about the essence of the art of medicine, and the kind of ideas that a contemporary man or woman needs in order to begin the practical search for truth in the comtemporary culture.

18. The Staff of Hermes

In order to record the remainder of our conversation as compactly as possible, I shall eliminate all minor comments and asides that took place between us and present it in the form of a monologue. I have also taken the liberty of rearranging the sequence of the conversation so as to make clear the logical relationship of one thought to another. What this method loses in verisimilitude will, I hope, be outweighed by a gain in coherence such that I may justifiably consider this conversation to be the summing up and conclusion of this book. I ask the reader's indulgence if what follows sounds more like a lecture than a conversation. In fact, it did become the lecture that I delivered to a small audience of physicians shortly after leaving here. The full title of this lecture was, "The Two Serpents of Hermes: The True Physician as the Archetype of Man."

I began, "I need to explain to you first why I started writing to your uncle. Obviously, you realize that my interest is not only in medicine. No, the question that has been gnawing at me is something more universal, which can be put very simply: what is the real difference between human beings? What is it that makes one person superior to another, I mean superior in reality and not just according to subjective preferences or according to hypocritical cliches about morality and so-called virtue. What is the root of great ability and skill in a human being?—the power to do the right thing and really do it well.

"As I say, this question in one form or another had interested me for many years, but for a long time it had remained merely philosophical for me. Even when I was very young and when everything else in the Bible was more or less meaningless to me, I was struck by the words in the book of Job: 'What is man that thou are mindful of him?' But the reason that these words made such an impression on me was not so much that I wanted to know the answer to the question. What puzzled me most, even when I was really very young, was that it was a question at all. I used to think: Why should anyone have to ask such a question? I know what things are: This is an apple, that is a book, that is a stone, and we are just that—people.

"But when I was a college student and turned toward the study of philosophical ideas, I seized upon that very same question: What is the nature of man, what is the self? For a long time, I was especially drawn to the philosophy of Plato. There was something in his teaching that puzzled and attracted me in the same way as the question of the nature of man. And that was the word *Being*. What is Being? Again I thought, what a strange thing to ask! Why would anyone trouble about such a question?

"Of course, the question about *Being* also remained only philosophical, that is, mental, for a very long time. It's impossible to have any concept adequate to the word *Being*. Being? It is everything that is and . . . it is nothing at all. So, why not just forget about this word? I don't know why, but I could not go very far away from either of these questions—the nature of man and the nature of Being. Psychology and metaphysics.

"My life rolls on—writing books, teaching, raising a family. Within all that, I try, with help, to study myself in order to become the sort of man who in my quiet moments, I really wish to be. But although I become a professional expert in the history of philosophy and religion, and although I come to many new insights about the definition of man, I begin to realize that my most intimate nature still lies untouched and unchanged right beneath the surface of myself. I begin to understand that there is something about myself that lives without my conscious participation in it and that the word *being* is the only word that can be applied to it. I begin to understand that I have not come in touch with my own being. And I realize that neither science nor philosophy has brought any of us into contact with the being of nature or the universe.

"My career makes it necessary for me to associate with the most respected people in our society—artists, educators, scientists, religious leaders of every kind. Gradually, very slowly and very deeply, there begins to accumulate in me impressions of other people and of myself that bring me in front of a stark fact: that almost no one really knows how to do anything, no one understands the whole of what they do—or, rather, of what is done through them.

"At first, this impression took the form of the feeling that the world had all at once become incompetent. I had the sense that suddenly teachers no longer knew how to teach—although something called teaching was taking place; scientists no longer knew how to observe or think or even to conduct experiments—although something called scientific discoveries were being made at an ever increasing tempo; religious leaders no longer knew how to touch the hearts of their followers—although religious organizations of all kinds were growing in numbers and strength.

"I began to feel like an inverted version of Alice in Wonderland or like a Socrates going around Athens trying to discover someone who really understood something and finding no one. You remember how he went to the poets, the political leaders, the craftsmen, and the scientists and saw that in everyone's activities things just did themselves through them without anyone really understanding the essence of their work or their own lives.

"But this whole state of affairs struck me with the greatest force only when I began to speak to doctors. Perhaps it was because at just that time I was beginning to have the most poignant impressions that my own activities suffered from the same malaise, that my own work as a teacher and writer and that my whole life suffered from the same malaise. Or perhaps it was because of the strong emotional associations I have always had, since childhood, about the stature of the physician as a special kind of individual. Whatever the cause, when I began speaking to doctors and observing their work, I was stunned by the combined impression of technological achievement and the personal lack of intrinsic skill in the doctors themselves.

"By intrinsic skill, I mean to refer to something rather different than a particular ability to do this or that thing. I don't mean manual dexterity or intellectual expertise or anything of that kind. Because there certainly were gifted surgeons, able diagnosticians, brillant specialists among the doctors I met and studied. And there were others who were able to strike up a good rapport with their patients—although there were far fewer of these than I had expected. But I am not speaking about the performance of these specific activities. That is, I soon saw that all these activities were techniques and I was fairly struck by what a technique really is: a procedure accomplished with mechanical attention.

"When I say that doctors now have much technique but very little intrinsic skill, I mean that the organic, intuitive intelligence is dying in them while the acquired automatisms of merely mental knowing are spreading like a cancer. The mental automatisms of technique are basically part of a passive force in man and, like a computer, are at the disposal of any passing impulse or desire either in us or outside of us. Without a presiding inner intelligence, these automatisms are blind, like an inanimate machine. They do good only by accident.

"By the way, did you know that the word *intelligence* is derived from words that mean 'to have force in oneself'?

"I will skip ahead a few steps and say now what I understood from my meeting this morning with Dr. Kaufman. I was not surprised to see that he has in himself that specific quality that is shared by people who are what might be called 'natural healers.' I was not surprised to sense this quality as a distinct vibration, an actual material force. I'm rather sure of this and I should add that I am very suspicious of all the dreaming and fantasying that nowadays goes on about so-called forces and vibrations. Mostly, people who speak like this are only imagining things. I can only tell you that in the case of your uncle, I am absolutely certain of what I perceived.

"As I say, I was not surprised to sense this quality in him. Thinking about him over the past two years and comparing my memories of him to the impressions I was receiving of doctors I was meeting and observing, I came to the conclusion that he had this sort of quality, intrinsically. But what surprised me very much was something I understood, in part by direct seeing and in part by logical speculation, about the nature of this special vibration or energy. What I'm trying to say is that I realized that this vibration is *intelligent*!

"And now, having said that, I am somewhat at a loss as to how to express myself further. My mind is overflowing with thoughts that emanate from being with your uncle this morning. I don't want to give you the impression that I'm making too much of a brief meeting with him and so I want to say again that a hundred, a thousand lines of questioning that I have been concerned with all my life, all came together in a sort of instantaneous vision when I was with him. I don't know to what extent I can unpack that moment in words now. But I will try.

"I don't know how Dr. Kaufman acquired this faculty of being a natural healer, which I am sure he possessed even when I first knew him. How a man acquires this kind of energy I don't know. Perhaps some people are born with it. Perhaps they acquire it by means of great suffering that they have undergone with a special sort of attitude . . .

"Ah, I see from your face that you know something in his life, some kind of suffering when he was younger? I want to know about that, but please let me go on for now.

"This energy or vibration that a natural healer possesses acts on the instinctual mind of the patient. I say 'instinctual mind' with special emphasis. I don't say merely, 'instinct,' a word that we usually use to mean something that acts without perceptions. The body has a mind. The body *is* a mind. And what *we* call mind is not at all the same thing. Our thoughts, our thinking processes, our logic and judgments, operate with quite a different kind of energy, which can have no direct influence on the organic, instinctual processes either in ourselves or in another human being. Our ordinary minds have no direct power over the instintual mind that is the human body. All great systems of knowledge have spoken of this as regards the way our lives are conducted, with the impulses of the body really ruling us. But it is true as well on the internal organic level. Our thoughts can jerk our bodies around in a crude external way but can have no inner power over the instinctual, biological forces moving within the body.

"Only an energy that corresponds to the energy of instinct can influence the body from within. Only a mind with a force at least equal to the intelligent energy of the body can influence the body from within. In illness, it seems to me, the instinctual mind needs energy so that the process of self-healing can proceed. The physician can give or, rather, call forth that energy that exists somewhere within the body in a kind of reservoir. And it is here that the role of emotion enters, which represents even another kind of energy within us. But let me speak of that later . . .

"Dr. Kaufman has some of that force within him, of this I have no doubt. Great physicians always have it and have had it throughout history in all times and cultures. We do not recognize it in our science nowadays, and where it is spoken of in unorthodox medicine, one despairs of finding the scientific precision necessary to do more than stumble upon it accidentally and afterwards merely to imagine things about it. It can be understood in such a foolish way that the idea of this energy causes far more harm than good, encouraging people to dream of healing without accepting the medical treatment, external though it may be, that is available.

"This external kind of treatment that proceeds on the basis of logical deductions and ordinary sense-observation is indispensable, and it is such treatment that modern medicine has developed through the application of scientific theory and method. I am sure that if the legendary Asclepius existed, even he had need of an accumulation of external information and observation. There are strictly mechanical, machinelike aspects of the human body that function quite passively and automatically. One needs knowledge of this passive aspect of the body.

"Modern science gives us knowledge and information about the automatic aspect of nature and the universe. It does not intend to and can never succeed in giving us knowledge of the active forces in the universe, forces to which the terms *conscious, intentional,* and *purposive* can truly be applied. It is wrong to try to wring this kind of knowledge from science or to blame it for not providing us with it. About the human body, therefore, science also gives us knowledge only of its passive or automatic aspects. It is wrong to blame modern medicine for not giving us knowledge of a kind that it cannot possibly provide.

"As I understand it, in order to fully treat certain diseases, it is necessary to deal with both forces in the human body. In certain cases, dealing with only one or another force will succeed or will succeed to a limited extent, enough to support the continued functioning of the organism. But in other cases, and in all cases where a complete healing is sought, it is necessary to bring both the active and the passive forces within the body into their proper balance.

"The active forces of the body can be evoked or supported by an active energy coming from without. The physician as healer is precisely the channel for this external support. There can be other people who are channels for this energy—call them healers, as well, if you wish. But the term *physician* must be reserved for a human being who is both a channel for this active energy and who also has external knowledge and information in the intellect, as well as a trained and dextrous physical capability that enables him to perform the necessary manipulations upon the body of the patient.

"The physician must also have a special sensitivity, a specially developed ability to perceive, sense, and feel what is being manifested by the patient. But here, too, there are many possibilities that can easily be confused with one another. There are healers who are not physicians and who seem to have this special kind of intuitive sensitivity. But the fact is that without the necessary intellectual knowledge, such healers often give wrong explanations and apply wrong labels to what they perceive. And yet, they often succeed in helping the patient. I interpret this situation in the following way: The active energy manifests itself through a sensitivity of perception; it is an intelligent energy. These perceptions by the natural healer are forms by which the healing or active energy passes into the patient. These intuitive perceptions are not knowledge in the full sense of the term. The mistake here is to conclude that the natural healer, who is not a physician, really understands something. Most often, he does not. He is simply a channel. But it is equally wrong to conclude that because the natural healer does not have knowledge, he is always a charlatan, or to conclude that there is no such thing as a healing force that one human being transmits, as it were, to another.

"The authentic physician is both a healer and a man of knowledge. That is, he has within himself a balance of two kinds of power: a strong life-energy and a well-developed intellect. If these two aspects of his being are not in some kind of balance, he is not a physician. Vital energy without a developed mind can produce results only haphazardly and can sometimes bring about more harm than good. A developed intellect without vital energy cannot directly affect the self-healing forces in the patient and can therefore only lead to temporary and often superficial results in treatment, and only for those patients whose illnesses are mechanical rather than organic.

"Please allow me to go on and to go a bit further into speculation and generalization. In my view, when Dr. Kaufman was younger, these two sides of his nature were more in correspondence. I cannot be as precise about this as I would wish. I don't undersand enough and so I have to fall back on a bit of philosophizing here. I could say, speaking very loosely, that when he was a younger doctor, his scientific mind was in some kind of relationship to his power as a healer. He knew less, perhaps, but what he knew was not too far away from this vital, intelligent energy within him. This energy, or vital mind, could express itself not only by a direct material action on the body and mind of his patients but could also to some extent select the thought associations in his own mind. This is *intuition* in its real meaning, as opposed to false intuition that is only an emotional impulse blindly evoking chance thought associations and investing them with egoistic assurance.

"I am presumptuous enough to speculate that as time passed,

Dr. Kaufman's knowledge departed more and more from this vital energy within him. Of course, now it is quite a different story. I needn't tell you what an exceptional man he is now. I will not even try to speculate how that has happened, since I don't know what it can mean to be facing one's own death, what it shows a man, what it can bring together in certain individuals.

"But I am saying that with the passage of time, the Dr. Kaufman I knew went out further and further into the proliferation of mental knowledge, new methodologies, new technologies, the explosion of data, the fragmentation of specialized information. In addition, he went out further and further into the changing forms of medical practice that have developed in our society due to the industrialization of health care and the general bureaucratization of all mutual human relations. These societal pressures together pulled him away from any access to the sources in himself that enabled the manifestation of his gifts as a natural healer. The two kinds of energy within him, the self-sensing energy and the energy of thought, moved further and further away from each other. You could say that his personality developed at the expense of his essence. These terms are not my own invention; they come from the teaching of Gurdjieff, and, since I have mentioned the name of Gurdjieff, let me put this in his own words. Speaking of what happens when a man's mental knowledge loses its connection with his inner being, he said that such knowledge becomes abstract and inapplicable to the whole of life. It may even become actually harmful, because instead of serving life and helping people to struggle with the difficulties they meet, it begins to complicate man's life, brings new difficulties into it, new troubles and calamities that were not there before.

"I ask you, isn't this an exact characterization of our whole modern culture? For every difficulty that is solved through the application of scientific knowledge, two new difficulties are created that require more inventions, more technology, which in turn spawn more and more difficulties and complications. There is nothing active within us that can select what is necessary and useful for the whole conduct of life; there is nothing active within us that can sense the whole aim and purpose of what we are doing, no instrinsic skill.

"As I have come to understand this, the whole of modern civilization represents a process of the development of knowledge out of all proportion to being, and it is this and this alone that explains the crisis of our era. The intellect of man, in its ordinary form, is the channel of a certain kind of force— there can be no question about that. But man was meant to embody and manifest the blending of all the fundamental forces in the universal world, not only one of them.

"Man was meant to be a creator, not a collection of thoughts and procedures attached to a balloon called ego. We know what creation is. It's all around us. It involves tremendous forces—the unimaginable forces of nature together with the unimaginable intelligence of nature. Nature's mind and nature's power are two unimaginably great realities that constantly blend together in life and separate in death. We feel this and sense this truth in our deepest moments of personal presence, but our thinking cannot comprehend it. Yet we are it—unconsciously, as is all of nature and all of existence.

"However, one question remains and it is the most serious question of all. These two forces in the greatness of nature— what brings them together and what moves them apart? What lives and moves in between the forces of creation? The ancient teachings gave many different names to this third force that me-diates the other two and that makes the universe one-in-many.

"But if one carefully studies the history of civilizations, one sees everywhere the gradual forgetting of this teaching about the third principle. It is a forgetting that occurs in human experience, in the living of life from day to day. Our own culture has been nearly ruined by this forgetting, which is expressed in the rigid dualism of the ideas of mind and matter. This is a philosophical error, but philosophical errors are not so serious. What is serious is the experiential forgetting of this truth.

"My head is overflowing with thoughts and I can't express them all at once. In such cases, a logical formulation can be of help as a platform from which to speak. Logically, conceptually, it can be said that there are three fundamental movements in nature—one movement proceeding from the Source outward; the second movement proceeding back toward the Source; the third moving in between these two.

"Modern knowledge, science as we know it, serves only one of these movements, the movement outward. And our own lives, such as they are, serve only this one force in nature. It is through the sensitivities of the body that the movement of return is sometimes experienced in ourselves, however. But we are unable to recognize this experience when it happens and unable to give it its proper name. We don't distinguish these exceptional experiences from the more familiar and common physical sensations. We don't see that these experiences of another force moving within the body are metaphysically distinct from even the most exquisite sensations of well-being. We don't see that another kind of energy is at issue here. And at one of its levels, this different quality of energy, this movement of return, manifests itself outward as what we may call a special kind of vibration that, when mixed with other vibrations of the organism, is a kind of magnetism that can affect the physical, instinctual mind in another human being. As I understand it, the real meaning of healing lies here.

"A physician is a man in whom both these movements, the movement of return in the body and the movement outward in the intellect, are in some correspondence. A man who has both magnetism and conceptual knowledge. Similarly, an authentic human being is one in whom these two aspects of nature are in some degree of correspondence, whose inherent vital energy and learned behavior are in some balance. I would say, furthermore, that any culture that furthers the development of only one side, is bound to come to a destructive end sooner or later.

"But, as I say, this is only part of the story. There must be in man something that moves in between these two forces of nature, a presiding energy or intelligence. The potential for the existence within himself of this third principle is what distinguishes man among all the creatures of nature. Without this presiding energy, the intelligence and power of which exceeds the level of either side of his nature, the balance of two forces is unstable even in those rare moments when these two forces move closer to each other, or in those rare individuals who happen by chance to have in themselves a degree of correspondence between them.

"A physician in the truest sense of the term—and now I obviously mean a human being in the truest sense of the term—is not simply two beings, as the documents of the old religions seem to say. He is two-in-one, which means, actually, three. He is inner being and outer knowledge together in stable harmony. The force that enables this harmony is, properly speaking, what the ancient wisdom calls the true self, the true Man. And you may be interested to know that in ancient China this true man was actually called the Great Physician.

"But I am trying to say too much in too little time. I only speak in this way because of what you asked about the ideas that formed the background of my letters to your uncle.

"It all comes down to this: In my opinion, modern medicine, modern science, modern man has more knowledge than he can possibly use. Or, rather, he has a certain level of knowledge, a certain quality of knowledge composed of a mass of information and techniques in which he wanders as in a labyrinth. He cannot see the whole, he cannot feel what is essential and what is secondary in all this knowledge. Since it is knowledge plus vital energy that heals another, the more knowledge he obtains at the expense of acquiring access to the higher energies within himself, the worse his life and practice become. It has been said of modern medicine that it does not extend life, but merely prolongs death. This is an example of how knowledge out of relation to the force of conscience and intelligence makes life not better but worse. There are many such examples in modern medicine and in modern life as a whole.

"When I once asked someone whose wisdom I greatly respected the same sort of question you asked me, I was answered in one sentence that baffled me at the time. I was told: 'Strive for being, all else will follow.' I believe I can paraphrase that statement, if I may, with a gnomic statement of my own: 'When doctors become men, then men will become doctors.'"

With that remark, Dr. Schira and I both laughed. I heaved a long sigh and drank some cold coffee.

19. What Are We Searching For?

It was already late in the afternoon and as the conversation drew to an end, I began to hope that Dr. Kaufman would come down the stairs so that I could see him once more before I left. As if reading my thoughts, Dr. Schira informed me that her uncle always rested throughout the afternoon and did not appear again until the early evening when he took a light supper and worked at his papers. Hearing that, I was reminded of my own obligations for the evening and realized with a slight start that I had not prepared at all for the lecture I was scheduled to give.

Still, it was not yet time for me to leave. We both knew that. There was still something that needed saying and each time I made a move to get up, Dr. Schira held me back with a remark, a question, a further observation. Finally, when we had really run out of peripheral things to say, she fell silent and fixed her glance on the table in front of her. She made an unusual gesture with her hands as though she were holding a large ball and weighing it. Then she placed both hands palm down on the table and looked at me. Once again, she seemed remarkably young and vulnerable but full of intention and purpose.

I understood her state very well. This is the state that may be called, and has been called, "the first step."

Looking at her, I had these thoughts:

This person is the best of her generation and therefore also the best of her profession. And what is that "best"? It is an awareness of lack, of need. All that the calling of the physician has represented throughout the centuries has vanished from view. It still exists, this calling, but it has retreated into the realm of the invisible, waiting for real men and women to allow its reappearance.

I recalled something that Dr. Schira had told me about her uncle's visits to the Middle East, where he had met with some of the practitioners of the traditional medicine there, the *hakims* or "wise men" of the old Persian culture. Apparently, he had spent some time with an especially interesting *hakim*, who was also known as an "alchemist" and who described at length how he prepared several of his medicines. He had spoken of forty steps in the preparation of one of these medicines, how each step, each decantation had to be made with the utmost care and sensitivity, and, so I surmised, with the utmost awareness of one's own inner state of attention. This was a very old man around whom numerous younger people gathered. But he ended by confessing to Dr. Kaufman that he had not found anyone to whom he could pass on his knowledge and that when he died, his knowledge would die with him.

Looking at Dr. Schira, I understood that something comparable had happened in our own culture as well. There was simply no way that Dr. Schira could now directly receive the magnetism of the *role* of the physician. Nothing of that power, borrowed though it is at the outset, could fall upon her shoulders. And how recently every last shred of that power had disappeared from our culture! This was really and truly a first generation of men and women, a first generation of physicians—and, in fact, of every role in human life: doctor, artist, teacher, mother, father, everything.

I saw how true it was to say that our world has actually passed through some kind of major shift, taken some fundamental step— up or down, down probably. It was no longer quite true to say that we were living in an age of transition. We have passed through the transition. It is over. It is a new world. Better or worse? I don't know, worse probably, but better too if the quality in the person in front of me was any indication.

Dr. Schira wore her role like an ill-fitting, external garment. She was born seeing through the falsities and automatisms that had devoured the physician's role in the modern world. She could no longer wish to be a physician; she could only wish to be a human being.

It is a new world. 1984 has come and gone and the world is neither as good as had been hoped nor as bad as had been feared. It is neither the new world of the believers in scientific progress, the fully explained world dreamt of in the early decades of this century, nor is it the totalitarian world-state foreseen by the Orwells and Huxleys and the visionary artists of the nineteenth century.

A new world, in which one could no longer play out the old scripts and in which the new scripts had not yet been written. It was a world in which the most real feeling was the sense of lack, the impression of confusion.

When Dr. Schira finally spoke what was on her mind, it struck me with the inevitability of a natural law. It was not only the question of her generation of men and women; it was the question of our whole culture: "How can I find what you are speaking of? How should I look for it?"

It is now clear to me that in that question lies the beginning of a new basis of morality and ethics for our time. The question is not what is the truth? but, rather, how to search for the truth? Not what is the good? but, rather, how to search for the good?

A fundamental reevaluation of values is at stake here. In this new world we see something about our human condition that has not been seen clearly enough in the whole history of the modern era. We see that it is impossible for us to be what we wish to be, to act as we would wish to act. The moral principles that have been handed down to us can have no power in our lives. The roles we are called upon to play are too big for us; they are as though designed for larger beings than we are.

It has been this way for a long time, well before this present era. But now we see it without any possibility of error. We can do nothing and we can be nothing. It has all vanished, every trace, as we stare blankly at the possible future that our mistakes have painted for us—annihilation, robotization, insectification of human life amid artificial air, artificial gravity, artificial worlds.

But we can search. The new cultural hero is the Seeker; he is the only real mythic symbol of our time. The Warrior? But who is he to fight against? Who are the evil enemies? There are none, because there is nothing simple and good that we can feel—we have no clear, simple, organically powerful feelings for what is good; therefore we have no clear enemies. The Rebel? But what is there to rebel against? If we could feel that there was something external to overcome, then everything might be different. Our modern rebels, the revolutionary with his absurdly literal lethal bombs turns to violent emotions as an obscure substitute for the passion of human feeling; agitation has usurped the place of will, which is a quiet, finely vibrating energy far above the obsessions of the ego. The Saint? The Sage? The Artist/Creator? These are now fantasies, not symbols that can move us to practical action. Between the Saint, the Sage, the Warrior, the Rebel, the Artist, and all the other symbols of other times—between these archetypal symbols and ourselves there now lies a great interval to be crossed, a gap, a chasm over which there stretches a swaying narrow footbridge. Who will cross it? The Seeker.

Like all these ancient symbols, which have now become dreams, the dream of the Great Physician is a measure of our lack, a script that no one can perform.

I asked Dr. Schira to make more coffee. I still had two hours before I was scheduled to deliver my lecture.

When she returned, we spoke uninterruptedly about the path I had been following for so many years. I found it extraordinary how all the ideas and practical methods that had been such a help to me came together in my own mind because I was with someone who had the great wish to know and understand. I saw how everything I had been given could all be understood as conditions for seeking. And what exactly, was I—were we—searching for? Not anything that could be easily named—not exactly wisdom, not exactly truth, not exactly freedom as definable concepts. Something else—something simple and immensely difficult: the transformation of the seeker himself. We spoke of a search that could be of such intensity and guided with such precision that the study of oneself as one is would become the principal means of transformation. That which aided this search was good; that which hindered it was bad. There was for us no other real meaning to good and bad, because only out of this transformation could a man or woman hope to find the energy to be, to love, to create, to choose, to help my suffering neighbor.

When Dr. Schira and I finally parted, we did so with the understanding that we would see each other again and speak further about the work of self-study. She said again that she felt my letters were written not to Dr. Kaufman, but to her. I nodded in agreement.

It was already getting dark outside. As I was unlocking the car door, I noticed a light go on on the second floor of Dr. Kaufman's house. I stood by the car for a few minutes watching the shadow of a man passing back and forth over the curtained window. I waited. Soon, as I knew it would, the curtain parted. Dressed in a bright blue robe, Dr. Kaufman looked out the window and down at me. I felt sorrow catching at my throat and then a great joy, as when I stood by him at the death of my grandfather.